What Would the Founders Do?

Also by Richard Brookhiser

The Outside Story:
How Democrats and Republicans Re-Elected Reagan

The Way of the WASP:
How It Made America, and How It Can Save It ... So to Speak

Founding Father: Rediscovering George Washington

Rules of Civility:
The 110 Precepts That Guided Our First President in War and Peace

Alexander Hamilton, American

America's First Dynasty: The Adamses 1735–1918

Gentleman Revolutionary:
Gouverneur Morris, The Rake Who Wrote the Constitution

What Would the Founders Do?

Our Questions, Their Answers

Richard Brookhiser

BASIC
BOOKS

A Member of the Perseus Books Group
New York

Copyright © 2006 by Richard Brookhiser

Published by Basic Books
A Member of the Perseus Books Group

Books published by Basic Books are available at special discounts for
bulk purchases in the United States by corporations, institutions, and
other organizations. For more information, please contact the
Special Markets Department at the Perseus Books Group,
11 Cambridge Center, Cambridge MA 02142, or call (617) 252-5298
or (800) 255-1514, or e-mail special.markets@perseusbooks.com.

Design by Jane Raese
Text set in 12-point Adobe Caslon

A CIP catalog record for this book is available from the Library of Congress.
ISBN-10: 0-465-00819-4
ISBN-13: 978-0-465-00819-3

06 07 08 09 / 10 9 8 7 6 5 4 3

For
Paul Russo

Contents

A Note on Spelling

Benjamin Franklin wanted Printers to capitalize the first Letters of all Nouns. This suggestion was not adopted, but many other changes occurred in the rules of spelling and punctuating between the founders' lifetime and ours. I have mostly retained their spelling, while modernizing their punctuation.

CHAPTER 1

Introduction

WHO CARES what the founders would do? Who believes that the experiences, opinions, or plans of men who lived two hundred years ago could have any relevance to our problems? Who imagines that the founders could answer our questions?

We do. I have heard it with my own ears. Over the past decade, I have given hundreds of talks about the founding fathers, on radio and TV, and to live audiences. Every time there is an opportunity for Q&A, there is at least one question of the form, "What would *Founder X* think about *current event,* or *living person, Y*?" No subject is too trivial, no problem too difficult. Audiences want to know what the founders would do about guns, taxes, race, the war on drugs, the war in Iraq; about Newt Gingrich, Bill Clinton, George W. Bush. A recent talk about Alexander Hamilton, first treasury secretary, and first (and so far only) former treasury secretary to be shot, was typical. The host was a financial services firm on Park Avenue. The crowd was young to middle-aged, white collar—white shirtsleeve, on their lunch break. Out of two hundred people, a dozen asked questions. Four wanted Hamilton's opinion about a contemporary issue: the balance of trade, recent decisions of the Supreme Court on federalism, the New York Stock Exchange, and the tone of modern politics (the presidential campaigns of 2000 and 2004 were fresh in everyone's mind). The man had been dead for two centuries; the duel he died in is still the most familiar thing about him (that, and his rather *GQ*-ish portrait on the ten-dollar bill). Yet a crowd whose business is to anticipate tomorrow's business wanted to know what he would think about the stories that were on that day's Bloomberg.

Americans have been asking what the founders would do since the founders died. In 1860 Abraham Lincoln kicked off his first presidential campaign with a speech at Cooper Union in New York City—a combined equivalent of an Iowa caucus and an appearance on *Oprah*. Lincoln's issue was whether the federal government could regulate slavery in the territories—the unsettled interior of the continent, not yet divided into states. The Supreme Court (in the *Dred Scott* decision) had said no; Lincoln said yes. At Cooper Union he spent half his debut talk examining what the thirty-nine signers of the Constitution thought about federal regulation of territorial slavery. He concluded that twenty-one of them, including George Washington, agreed with him (perhaps two disagreed; sixteen had no provable opinion). He wrapped himself in Washington. We "sustain his policy. . . . [Y]ou [that is, the supporters of slavery] repudiate it."

Lincoln won the election; the Civil War began. In 1863, in the Gettysburg Address, he wrapped the Union cause in two founding documents. The first was the Declaration of Independence:

the moment (1863 minus four score and seven equals 1776) when Congress stated that "all men are created equal." The second was the Constitution, "government of the people, by the people, and for the people," which Lincoln hoped would not perish from the earth, echoing "We the People" who had established that government in the first place.

In the 1930s, with the world mired in the Depression, and various fascisms on the march, Franklin Roosevelt turned to Thomas Jefferson as to a touchstone. In 1938 Jefferson went on the nickel, in place of the Indian brave; Monticello went on the reverse, in place of the buffalo. FDR laid the cornerstone of the Jefferson Memorial the following year. The completed structure was dedicated in 1943, in the midst of World War II (the cherry trees on the Tidal Basin that so beautifully frame it in the spring had been a gift of the City of Tokyo in better times).

Twenty years after the Jefferson Memorial was finished, Martin Luther King Jr. gave his "I have a dream" speech in front of the Lincoln Memorial. He not surprisingly held up Lincoln and the Emancipation Proclamation as models for future black progress. But he also held up Lincoln's predecessors, "the architects of our republic," who when they "wrote the magnificent words of the Constitution and the Declaration of Independence . . . sign[ed] a promissory note to which every American was to fall heir." Many of the architects of the Republic, he knew, owned black men; some of them slept with black women they owned. But King laid claim to their words, not as a clever debater stealing rhetorical bases, but as a family member presenting a keepsake. He did not put the founders' words to his purposes; he found their purposes anticipating his words.

From the sublime to the ridiculous. When Bill Clinton was being impeached for lying under oath about his affair with an intern, his defenders claimed the founders as his role models, for DNA tests had just revealed that a Jefferson fathered one of the children of Thomas Jefferson's slave Sally Hemings, a tale that had been whispered about since Jefferson's years in the White House, whereas Alexander Hamilton, during his years as treasury secretary, had carried on an affair with Maria Reynolds, wife of a common crook, to whom Hamilton had paid blackmail—a tale on which whispering ceased the moment Hamilton revealed it in a ninety-five-page pamphlet, with the deceptively dull title *Observations on Certain Documents*. What was a little obstruction of justice next to paying blackmail and fathering a child on one's property? Clinton's enemies complained that Hamilton, at least, had told the truth about what he had done.

From the ridiculous to mass murder. After the destruction of the World Trade Center, exhausted firemen, cops, and rescue workers snatched scattered hours of rest on the pews of St. Paul's Chapel, an eighteenth-century Episcopalian church across the street from the hell hole. Among the pews they rested on is the one where George Washington worshiped after his first inauguration as president in 1789. Washington knew New York City well. It was there, in July 1776, that he had the Declaration of Independence read to his troops. And it was there, a few months later, that he tried to beat off a British invasion—the last time, before 9/11, that New York was attacked. Washington had a worse time of it than we did. The enemy chased him from the city, occupied it for seven and a half years, and let eleven thousand American soldiers die in filthy prison ships moored in the East River.

In moments of struggle, farce, or disaster, the founders are still with us. We look to them for slogans, cheap shots, inspiration, and instruction. We seize on them for sleazy advantage and for moral guidance. We ransack what they said and did for clues to what they would, and what we should, do.

The founders knew they were making history. John Adams believed that the day of independence "will be celebrated, by succeeding Generations, as the great anniversary Festival. . . . It ought to be solemnized with Pomp and Parade, with Shews, Games, Sports, Guns, Bells, Bonfires and Illuminations from one End of this Continent to the other from this Time forward forever more." Like every other country, we honor our heroes, celebrate our holidays, remember our defeats, and regret our failings. But we do more. We engage the founders in a continuing dialogue about the present. It is an imaginary dialogue, for the founders are dead. Yet they are not entirely dead, for they live on in our minds. Parades and fireworks commemorate American independence, as Adams predicted. But the *New York Times* also commemorates it by reprinting the Declaration of Independence. We are not content to remember what the founders did; we must read, or at least see, their explanation of it. Having read it, we feel that we can engage it. The Declaration is a position paper and an action memo that is always in our mailbox; we believe we can hit the reply button for further elaboration.

Our feelings about these historical figures seem more religious than historical. Evangelical Christians put the bumper sticker WWJD on their cars: What Would Jesus Do? The phrase comes from a religious novel, *In His Steps*, in which a minister in a middle American city asks his congregation to reform their lives by doing nothing "without first asking the question, 'What would Jesus do?'" The phrasing is borrowed, tongue in cheek, for the divinities of lesser faiths (WWMD—What Would Martha [Stewart] Do?). Yet the founders are not gods. "Had he lived in the days of idolatry," wrote Francis Hopkinson, a signer of the

Declaration, of George Washington, "he had been worshipped as a god." High praise. But Hopkinson, Washington, and the other founders believed they lived after the days of idolatry. When Jefferson and John Adams died on the same day, July 4, 1826, the fiftieth anniversary of the Declaration, Adams's oldest son, John Quincy Adams, saw the coincidence as a "visible and palpable mark . . . of Divine favor, for which I would humble myself in grateful and silent adoration before the Ruler of the Universe." God blessed the founders; they did not bless themselves. Their specialness comes from being human creators of a human thing, America. We, their successor Americans, feel simultaneously awed by them and like them. They built the country, they wrote the user manuals—Declaration, Constitution, *Federalist Papers*—and they ran it while it could still be returned to the manufacturer. We assume that if anyone knows how the U.S.A. should work, it must be them. In that spirit, we ask WWFD—What Would the Founders Do?

The question makes sense to us because the United States is still a relatively new country. Europe as we know it took shape in the Dark Ages—Charlemagne, Alfred the Great, Germans hammering at the Roman Empire. The Middle East looks back to Mohammed, and could look back to the Sphinx if it chose. India was old when Alexander the Great invaded it. China is older still. The maps are always changing, but the continuities go back a dozen centuries, or millennia. Our founding, by contrast, is only just beyond our fingertips. When I was in college I attended a lecture by Alger Hiss, the communist spy. When Hiss was a young man, he clerked for Justice Oliver Wendell Holmes Jr. When Holmes was a young officer in the Civil War, he scolded President Lincoln, who was visiting the front lines, for unwisely showing himself over a parapet. When Lincoln was in his late thirties, he served in the House of Representatives with former president John Quincy Adams. When Adams was a boy, he heard the cannon of the Battle of Bunker Hill from his family's house in Braintree. It is a short walk from the Revolution to this page—five degrees of historical separation. Even tacking on our colonial history does not make us that much older. When the Pilgrims landed, the Spaniards had already been in Mexico for a hundred years.

At the same time, our new country has unusually old institutions. The presidency and the Supreme Court go back to 1789. The army goes back to 1775 (a year before there was a country). Congress first met in 1774. Older countries, perhaps more confident of their identity, burn through their institutions with the insouciance of high-living heirs. In 1777 Louis XVI entered into an alliance with the United States, an embattled one-year-old. In July 1789, three months after Washington's first inauguration, the Bastille was stormed (the Marquis de Lafayette sent Washington the key), and a few years after that the king was deposed and executed. Louis was followed by five republics, two empires, two kingdoms, and fascism. In November 1797 when the first American ambassador to Prussia came to Berlin to present his credentials, the lieutenant who opened the city gates for him at night had never heard of the United States. Since then Germany has been a collection of independent countries, an empire, a republic, the Third Reich, and two republics, one of them a communist sham that was ultimately subsumed into the other. We are aged children, or sprightly oldsters. Our founders are close by, and they cast long shadows.

We are pleased with the shadows they cast. The founders as a group are intelligent, well spoken, and good company. Few of them were truly funny, but most of them appreciated a joke.

When they joined together to accomplish some task, the talent level could be humiliatingly high (humiliating to us, that is). George Washington's first cabinet was the strongest cabinet there has ever been, with Jefferson as secretary of state, Hamilton as secretary of the treasury, and Henry Knox as secretary of war. At a time when the population of the country was less than four million and everything west of the Alleghenies was bison, if you scraped the bottom of the barrel of the Washington administration, you found Henry Knox. Some barrel. The founders earn our affection, not only for who they were but also for what they were not. Major General Benedict Arnold committed treason, and former vice president Aaron Burr was tried for it, and acquitted. But neither Arnold's schemes nor Burr's, if he had any, bore fruit. One signer of the Declaration and two signers of the Constitution were killed in duels. But no founder died on a scaffold or in prison, the victim of some other founder's extralegal wrath or revenge. There were no coups or putsches in the founding, no guillotines, no purges, no devouring of its own.

We admire the founders most for their handiwork. The country they left seems to offer freedom, order, prosperity, and hope. If it doesn't offer these things, they are assumed as a promise—a promissory note, as King put it—that can be demanded. The resulting complacency of Americans, their satisfaction with their institutions or with the potential of their institutions, is of course the very thing that drives America's critics and enemies wild. Even American radicals can strike foreign radicals as cozy fakers, tinkering with half measures: Karl Marx dismissed his American followers as "middle class humbugs and worn-out Yankee swindlers in the Reform business" (they wanted to push for women's rights ahead of workers' power). Even when Americans become desperate enough to consider revolution they find it in their own past. Jefferson thought occasional rebellions were "a medicine necessary for the sound health of government." Gouverneur Morris wrote Jefferson that "the basis of our own Constitution"—and Morris ought to have known, since he wrote it—"is the indefeasible right of the people to establish it." We can remake ourselves, because the founding fathers told us we could. Of course, that justification makes America's critics wilder yet.

We feel entitled to cross-examine the founders because they were not divinity or royalty. They were men who became leaders because they were elected to their jobs, or because they were appointed by leaders who had been elected. Jefferson, Madison, and James Monroe, the third, fourth, and fifth presidents, were called the Virginia dynasty, but they were political soul mates, not blood relatives or even in-laws. John Adams's enemies accused him of wanting to found a House of Adams by marrying his eldest son to a daughter of George III; John Quincy Adams did follow his father into the White House, but he did it by winning the job, after marrying the daughter of an American merchant. The greatest citizens of a republic are still citizens. If we stop liking them, we can vote them out of office; if they stop obeying the law, they can be removed from office. At all times, they are accountable to other officers of government, or to the people. Death doesn't change the situation. Even when the founders reach heaven (or elsewhere) we feel we can buttonhole them. They ruled us, but they were like us; their shades are like us still.

The founders invite our questions now because they invited discussion when they lived. They were argumentative, expansive know-it-alls, hanging their ideas out to dry in public speeches and in journalism. Sometimes writing for the press wasn't enough for them; Benjamin Franklin and Samuel Adams founded newspapers; the newspaper Alexander Hamilton founded, the *New-York*

Evening Post, is still being published (minus *Evening* and the hyphen). Not everything they did was for public consumption, or discussion. They schemed behind closed doors, as all politicians do, and they issued sweeping pronouncements from on high, as proud and intelligent people often do. "I have written very dogmatically," said Fisher Ames at the end of one letter, describing the doings of the First Congress, "and why should I affect doubts, when I entertain none?" Yet since the founders also knew that the judges of their plans and their doings were the public, they constantly sought to show, demonstrate, persuade, or inspire. The Declaration submits itself to "the opinions of mankind." The *Federalist Papers* declare that their arguments "will be open to all and may be judged of by all." In a world of potentates, in which most rulers showed themselves only ceremonially and explained themselves seldom, where the first finance minister of France to publish a budget was dismissed for doing so, and where anyone who approached the emperor of China was obliged to kneel three times, touching the ground with the forehead, the founders were out there.

All their lives they had to say what they would do. So why should they get a rest when we need a little advice?

CHAPTER 2

Their World, Our World

WE INVITE the founders from their world to our world because we assume that the two worlds are similar. In many ways, we're right. But we need to carry, in our minds, a picture of their world, as a gauge for their likeness, and their otherness.

When we talk about America's founding, we are talking about two banner events: the American Revolution (from the Battle of Lexington in 1775 to the Treaty of Paris in 1783) and the creation of the Constitution (from the Constitutional Convention in 1787 to the ratification of the Bill of Rights in 1791). The founders were the people who starred in these shows (most of them men, though some women do come front and center from time to time). The lives of the founders stretch well over a century, from 1706, when Benjamin Franklin was born, to 1836, when James Madison died. But their relevant public careers fall, with only a few exceptions, in the six decades between the French and

Indian War, which George Washington started in 1754, and the War of 1812, which Madison won (if you could call it that) in 1815. One battle in the French and Indian War, Braddock's defeat in 1755, brought together these figures of the future: Thomas Gage, who would command the British army in Boston in 1775; Washington, who would command the American army opposing Gage; Horatio Gates, who would win the Battle of Saratoga; Charles Lee, who would almost lose the Battle of Monmouth; Daniel Morgan, who would win the Battle of Cowpens; and Daniel Boone, who would settle Kentucky. Benjamin Franklin, leader of the Pennsylvania Assembly, gave all these men their supplies. The political battles that raged during the War of 1812 involved these figures of the past: Madison, the father of the Constitution, who was for peace with honor, versus Gouverneur Morris, draftsman of the Constitution, who was for peace with dishonor (he wanted the United States to lose and to break apart).

Almost all of the founders were born in the future United States, the thirteen colonies of Great Britain in North America, which stretched from Maine (then part of Massachusetts) to Georgia. A handful had come to America from England, Scotland, or Ireland. One, the exotic Alexander Hamilton, came from the West Indies. A few freedom fighters who took a more-than-professional interest in the United States—Baron von Steuben, the Marquis de Lafayette—came from continental Europe. Two of them—Count Pulaski and Baron de Kalb—gave their lives here.

The world the founders lived in was larger than ours, because travel was slower, yet it was also smaller than ours, because people saw less of it. When the Continental Congress first met in Philadelphia in 1774, many of the delegates left home for the first

time. It took three days to get from New York City to Albany by
stage coach, and three days by sloop on the Hudson River, if the
wind was favorable (if the wind wasn't, the sloop could take two
weeks). Robert Fulton's steamboat began serving customers in
New York in 1807; Robert Livingston, signer of the Declaration,
was the chief investor. But it only ran up and down the Hudson.
Travel to the interior from the coast was miserable; the first
shovel of dirt for the Erie Canal was not turned until 1817. Benjamin Franklin watched the first balloon flight with human pas-
sengers outside Paris, and received the first airmail, a letter
addressed to him carried by balloonists across the English Chan-
nel, though only scientists and daredevils went aloft themselves.
The Atlantic Ocean could be crossed in twenty-plus days in fair
weather; Thomas Paine was blown among icebergs in the North
Atlantic on one voyage and did not make it across for eighty
days.

Travel was uncertain as well as slow. John Adams, bound for
France, landed instead in Spain and had to finish his trip over-
land. Henry Laurens, another France-bound diplomat, was captured at sea by the British and thrown in the Tower of London.
Staying in America was no guarantee that you would get to your
destination: First Lady Abigail Adams's coachman got lost on
the way from Massachusetts to Washington, D.C. Given these
difficulties, some Americans made long trips, even extended
journeys of several years, but they made only a few. As a young
man Washington went to Barbados with his half brother, who
was hoping the Caribbean air would cure his tuberculosis (it
didn't). Thomas Jefferson, who spent four years as minister to
France, took one trip to Provence and pushed on into Italy as far
south as Genoa, where he admired the strawberries. Gouverneur
Morris, who spent nine years as a man about Europe, got as far

east as Vienna, where he noted the prostitutes. "A great number of women of the town" attended midnight mass, "also some of higher rank, and lower principles."

In terms of miles logged, the founders were less cosmopolitan than middle-class high school or college kids, who spend summers or semesters abroad, less worldly than soldiers and marines who serve in Afghanistan or Iraq. But like us, and unlike almost everyone before them in human history, they knew of the whole world. There were many blank spaces in the interiors of continents, but the globe had been circumnavigated numerous times. In the 1760s and 1770s Captain Cook filled in the last great gaps of the Pacific, discovering Australia, New Zealand, and Hawaii. The world supported a world economy. There were British merchants in Madras and Portuguese merchants in Macao; Russians harvested otters in Alaska, and Spaniards mined silver in Bolivia. Robert Morris, merchant and financier, sent the first American trading ship to China in 1784. Tens of thousands of slaves went yearly from Africa to the West Indies and America, and many thousands of dollars of sugar, rice, and tobacco went east from the West Indies and America to Europe.

The founders' lives were hemmed by diseases that were little understood. Two summertime yellow fever epidemics struck Philadelphia in the 1790s. Dr. Benjamin Rush, signer of the Declaration, treated his patients by draining their excess blood, in the process weakening them so that he killed most of them. When a journalist said so in print, Rush sued for libel and won, but that was only because the officers of the court were his friends. Alexander Hamilton, who came down with yellow fever while serving as treasury secretary, consulted Dr. Edward Stevens, a childhood friend from the West Indies, rather than Rush. Stevens understood yellow fever no better than Rush did, but at least his remedies—quinine, cold baths, brandy—did Hamilton no harm.

One scourge that medicine was getting a handle on was smallpox. A primitive form of inoculation, which involved purging the patient with emetics, deliberately inducing the disease, then giving him rest and a diet of milk, bread, and rice, was practiced in New England as early as the 1720s. One in forty who took the cure died, as opposed to the one in twelve who died from normal smallpox. John Adams took the cure, along with some friends, as a young man. He described the vomiting in a letter to his fiancée, Abigail Smith. "When my Companion was sick I laughed at him, and when I was sick he laughed at me. Once however . . . we were both sick together, and then all Laughter and good Humour deserted the Room." When Adams finally emerged from confinement, he celebrated by eating thirty oysters chased with Malaga. As the eighteenth century ended, the English doctor Edward Jenner invented a safe vaccination based on the nonlethal cowpox. When he was president, Jefferson wrote Jenner an eloquent tribute: "[M]ankind can never forget that you have lived."

By the founders' lifetimes, warfare had come to rely as much on gunpowder as on human muscle. Officers carried swords, and infantrymen were equipped with bayonets, which were useful in close fighting. But artillery, muskets, and a scattering of rifles did most of the killing; Native Americans preferred to use European weaponry when they could get it. Arrows and pikes were weapons of the past. When Thaddeus Kosciusko returned to his native Poland after the Revolution, he tried to defeat an invading army of Russians with a force of peasants carrying scythes. But that was a symptom of his desperation (he was overwhelmed). Warfare in North America was limited only by logistics. Europe's many roads and fertile fields made it possible to supply and feed armies much larger than the greatest forces that could be accumulated in America. The British expeditionary force that descended on New York Harbor in the summer of 1776 was one of the largest of the eighteenth century (thirty thousand men in ten battleships, and numerous smaller ships). They faced nineteen thousand men under George Washington. Even so, the two armies mustered only a fraction of the two hundred thousand men who had fought at the Battle of Malplaquet in what is now northern France in 1709.

Whatever the numbers involved, the scale of the wars the founders knew was as global as any war of the twentieth or twenty-first century. World War I was very late in the train of world wars. North America alone was a vast field of battle (the American Revolution was fought from Quebec to the West Indies, the War of 1812 from Montreal to New Orleans), and its fate was linked to international empires (Britain, France, and Holland) struggling in Europe and Asia. The sweep of these conflicts tempts historians to lurid eloquence. In King George's War (predecessor to the French and Indian War), wrote Macaulay, "black men fought on the coast of Coromandel [southwestern India] and red men scalped each other by the great lakes of North America." The Napoleonic Wars, wrote Henry Adams, were "a vast and bloody torrent which dragged America, from Montreal to Valparaiso, slowly into its movement." Back these words with a pounding theme and a montage of jump cuts and they could introduce a world news show today.

The wars that the founders fought in were inflamed by belief. As late as the Revolution, Americans still felt the dying glow of the religious wars of the seventeenth century. The Declaration of Independence criticized George III for upholding the benighted customs of Catholic Canadians ("He has . . . abolish[ed] the free system of English laws in a neighboring province"), whereas Benedict Arnold justified his treason by condemning America's alliance with Catholic France ("the enemy of the Protestant faith"). The wars ignited by the French Revolution, which would not end until Napoleon's last defeat at Waterloo, were embittered by the new faith of ideology. Political conviction, doing the work formerly reserved for creeds, gave perfect strangers thousands of miles apart common reasons for hating each other, and Americans, engaged in their own disputes, could pretend they were pseudo-Europeans, moved by the same arguments as French Jacobins or British Tories. The clash of civilizations was perfectly familiar to the founders.

The technology of everyday life was late medieval. Most Americans farmed; smiths, millers, and carpenters supplied their necessities beyond food. Luxuries—fur, rum, silk, gold, porcelain—came from the frontier, or abroad. But new modes of production were coming into being. In Britain, in the mid-eighteenth century, cotton cloth, once spun at home (hence its name, homespun), was produced in factories on water-powered spinning machines invented by Richard Arkwright. Britain's textile technology was so advanced, and so lucrative, that it was considered a state secret. British textile workers were forbidden by law from emigrating, lest they take their knowledge with them. But American businessmen tried to smuggle out models and experts. In 1789, Samuel Slater, an apprentice at a Derbyshire textile mill, sailed for New York disguised as a farmer. A year later he had joined forces with Moses Brown, an entrepreneur in Rhode Island, to set up a cotton-yarn mill. The long trek of manufacturing from the home and the artisan's shop to the factory floor had begun. A paradoxical effect of the early Industrial Revolution was to boost the market for slave labor, as the American South opened to cotton production.

The founders' generation saw a revolution in reading and discussion. Intelligent colonials of the late seventeenth and early eighteenth centuries felt marooned in an ocean of trees and indifference. The clergy of early New England were Cambridge-educated divines, who founded Harvard (1636) and Yale (1701) to train their sons and grandsons. Yet they thought of themselves as Zion exiled to the wilderness. Jonathan Edwards, the great preacher and theologian, wrote a wistful letter to a Scottish clergyman. "It might be of particular advantage to me here in this remote part of the world to be better informed of what books there are that are published on the other side of the Atlantic, and especially if there be anything that comes out that is very remarkable." Lewis Morris, an eccentric New Jersey landowner, amassed a private collection of three thousand books, of which he especially prized Tacitus. "Do not lend it on any account to anybody whatever, for I know that country [New Jersey] too well to lend books in. That is not a book fit come into a country fellow's hand, to daub and dirty." William Byrd II, of Westover, a clever, literate Virginia planter, spent thirty of his first fifty years living high in London. When he returned home, in 1726, he found himself "buried alive" in a "silent country." Byrd was not hearing the night silence of frog and whippoorwill, but the human silence of no one to understand his allusions or laugh at his jokes.

As the eighteenth century progressed, the silence lifted. It wasn't so much that more people were reading—colonial literacy had always been high—it was that more people knew other readers. Americans knew what other Americans read; in a sense, they were reading together. When Franklin was in his twenties, he founded the first public library in Philadelphia. "At the time I established myself in Pennsylvania there was not a good book-seller's shop in any of the colonies to the southward of Boston. In New York and Philadelphia the Printers . . . sold only paper, almanacs, ballads, and a few common school books. Those who loved reading were obliged to send for their books from England." Franklin persuaded his friends, who had formed a dis-cussion club, to store their books in a common room, "each of us being at liberty to borrow such as he wished to read at home." When that arrangement worked, Franklin thought of setting up a public subscription library. "So few were the readers at that time" that Franklin was at first able to corral only fifty sub-scribers. But the institution thrived, and other libraries appeared in other towns. "In a few years," travelers found Americans "bet-ter instructed and more intelligent than people of the same rank generally are in other countries."

The great diffuser of discussion was the press. Franklin was in on the ground floor of this phenomenon too. He got his first ex-perience on the *New England Courant*, a Boston paper founded by his older brother James. When he was sixteen years old young Franklin had to manage the *Courant* while James went to jail for suggesting that the town fathers colluded with pirates. After moving to Philadelphia, Franklin worked on newspapers there; his former apprentices founded papers in other towns. By the time of the Revolution, there were twenty-five newspapers in the thirteen colonies. The post office—another brainchild of the busy Franklin—made weekly versions of the most popular news-papers available throughout all the colonies. Americans who lived in towns had the modern media experience of simultaneity—learning of things almost as soon as they happened, at least when they happened at home. Their doings and their words gained a double existence by being reported and commented on. The experience whetted the desire to experience more.

The explosion of the press was all the more remarkable because hardly any other form of popular culture, high or low, existed. American literature was barbarous; America produced a few good painters, but they fled to London to practice their art (John Trumbull and Gilbert Stuart did return home). Professional actors and musicians straggled from town to town. Otherwise there was folk culture—people entertaining themselves. The one great exception was journalism, which existed in its modern form.

The founders lived in a small country—in 1776, America had about 2.5 million people, perhaps one-ninth the population of France, one-fifth the population of Britain. Philadelphia, the largest American city, had about 35,000 people, compared to 800,000 Londoners and 600,000 Parisians. But America was growing explosively. The population of the country in 1790 was 3.9 million, in 1800 5.2 million—in other words, it doubled in twenty-five years. Immigration accounted for some of the increase, but most of it came from reproduction. Franklin had thirteen siblings; Washington had eight. The founders' America was different from ours, a big country that is holding its own, though it was even more different from contemporary Europe, a big collection of countries that is aging and shriveling.

THAT WAS THE WORLD the founders lived in. What about the world that lived in them? What was in their minds?

Their minds were stuffed with recent British history. The seventeenth century in Britain had been a time of religious and political strife, an on-again, off-again civil war. King James I had almost been blown up by plotters, Charles I lost his head, and James II lost his throne. Americans remembered these conflicts; the colonies were dumping grounds for malcontents, as the fortunes of strife in Britain shifted. Three of the men who voted to execute Charles I fled to Connecticut when his son was restored to the throne; they were buried behind the Congregationalist church on the New Haven green. But at century's end, Britain arrived at a stable settlement of its differences. The king who replaced James II, William III, accepted the political primacy of Parliament, divided into a hereditary House of Lords and an elected House of Commons. The Church of England was recognized as the established national faith, but religious minorities, such as Catholics and Quakers, though penalized in various ways, were no longer hounded. Politicians abandoned warfare and coups in favor of factional fights; office and enrichment, not social or religious utopias, became the goals of statesmen. In the eighteenth century, the French philosopher Montesquieu— "the celebrated Montesquieu," Edmund Randolph called him at the Constitutional Convention—drew a constitutional theory of the separation of powers from British arrangements. Britons, at home and in America, studied his group portrait of themselves with pleasure. In their tripartite constitution—king, lords, and commons—they had found the magical balance between freedom and order.

The British consensus was not beyond criticism, however. Those who were out of power wondered if politics had been reformed enough. Perhaps the king and his ministers, though they did not assert a divine right to rule, as the kings of the seventeenth century had done, held as firm a grip on power by the earthly means of patronage and bribery. The most eloquent exponent of this view was Henry St. John, Viscount Bolingbroke, no liberal, but a right-wing opportunist with a journalist's flair for controversy and abuse. He was caustic, and he seemed principled; if he were alive today, he would blog. For decades he attacked the British establishment in books, essays, and a journal called the *Craftsman*. The price of liberty, he proclaimed, was eternal vigilance against crafty insiders. Washington owned a complete set of the *Craftsman*; John Adams realized that Bolingbroke was a bit of a fraud, but he still read him.

In the mid-eighteenth century another critic of the status quo appeared, the Scottish philosopher and historian David Hume. Hume was an atheist, a conservative, and an urbane and graceful writer, perhaps the only philosopher between Plato and Nietzsche who can be read for pleasure. Hume delighted in heresies. Corruption was not the shameful secret of the British system, but the grease that made the wheels turn. "Everyone knows," wrote Jefferson, that Hume's "charms of style" made his history of Britain "the manual of every student. I remember well the enthusiasm with which I devoured it when young, and the length of time, the research and reflection which were necessary to eradicate the poison it had instilled into my mind." Bolingbroke upheld the pieties of the day in their most extreme form, whereas Hume slyly undermined them. But both men seemed to offer useful practical advice, which unfortunately pulled in opposite directions: Hume told Americans how government works, and Bolingbroke told them that even when it works (especially when it works), it is to be distrusted.

During the late seventeenth and eighteenth centuries, the British invented the first political parties that were at all like modern ones; Whigs and Tories (who still exist), and the founders borrowed their names for their own disputes. British

Whigs tended to sympathize with America, before and even during the Revolution, whereas British Tories did the bidding of George III; American revolutionaries and loyalists were also called Whigs and Tories, respectively. Once the founders had created their own country, they created new parties, whose names can be confusing to us. In 1787–8, supporters of the Constitution were called Federalists; Alexander Hamilton, James Madison and John Jay wrote 85 pro-Constitution essays, the *Federalist Papers*, which are still read by high school students and justices of the Supreme Court. Opponents of the Constitution (Patrick Henry, George Clinton) were called Anti-Federalists. The more lasting parties that emerged in the 1790s were called Federalists and Republicans. Most of the Federalists of 1787–8 ended up in the Federalist Party, though not all: Madison helped found the Republican Party. The Federalist Party (George Washington, John Adams, Hamilton, Jay, Gouverneur Morris, Timothy Pickering) disappeared after 1816, leaving no heirs. The Republican Party (Thomas Jefferson, Madison, Clinton, James Monroe, Samuel Adams, Aaron Burr) became the modern Democratic Party, as the last founders were dying off; it has no connection to the GOP, which dates from the 1850s. The founders also called each other a variety of insulting names—Tories, Jacobins—which, like most abuse, had little meaning.

The British institution that Americans had the most contact with was the law. There were no law schools in the colonies or the early Republic. A few wealthy and ambitious Americans had studied at the Inns of Court in London. Most aspiring lawyers studied law with older practitioners before they were admitted to the bar. An occasional bright rustic, like Roger Sherman, a cobbler, surveyor, and almanac writer from Connecticut, taught himself law. The British common law was both old and ad hoc; it flowed, not from a scripture or one ancient lawgiver, but from an array of acts of Parliament and legal decisions that had been handed down over centuries. It offered both the patina of tradition and considerable freedom to maneuver. You scrambled for the best arguments you could find, then claimed that all history was on your side. The institution of the jury added elements of democracy and drama to trials. Lawyers had to know how to impress both judges and their fellow citizens. The most eloquent founders—Patrick Henry, John Adams—were skillful courtroom performers. Another psychological lesson the legal system taught, to lawyers at any rate, was that there is always another day, another case. If you lost, your client might be destroyed, but you would not. You might see the same judge again, and the same opposing counsel. You and your opposing counsel might be arguing the next case together, for a new common client.

Americans were steeped in the history of the ancient world, which to them consisted of Greece and Rome. (Freemasonry, introduced into America in the 1730s, claimed access to the wisdom of Solomon, but that was a secret tradition, not for public discussion.) Americans learned their ancient history in school; educational reformers periodically tried to tug learning out of its classical rut, but they failed, and young Americans went back to their Plutarch and Seneca, Cicero and Xenophon. Rome was both a great warning and a great example, for Rome had lost its liberties when the empire replaced the republic, yet Rome, under both republic and empire, had ruled the known world. Americans admired the achievement and hoped to avoid the failing. The first Caesars, Julius and Augustus, the would-be and actual subverters of the republic, were the focus of American fears and hopes. Augustus Caesar was the off-stage villain and temptation of the most popular play of the eighteenth century, Joseph Addi-

son's *Cato*. (Patrick Henry ["Give me liberty or give me death"]
and Nathan Hale ["I regret that I have but one life to give for my
country"] echoed lines from it.) Addison's hero was Cato the
Younger, a last beleaguered defender of the Roman republic. Although we admire Cato's nobility, against Caesar he is helpless.
As the play drives to its conclusion, one of Cato's followers, looking for silver linings, says that Caesar is after all humane. Cato's
response is sharp, and hopeless. "Curse on his virtues! They've
undone his country." Addison's play is forgotten, but the theme
of a usurping empire and a virtuous republic marches on, in *Star
Wars* and the chat rooms of the Left and Right.

Greece was less interesting to the founders, for it had given
the world much beauty and philosophy, but little in the way of
practical accomplishment. Alexander Hamilton put it bluntly: "It
is impossible to read the history of the petty republics of Greece
. . . without feeling sensations of horror and disgust at the dis-
tractions with which they were continually agitated." The most
beloved Greek in America was Plutarch, a second-century essayist. His *Parallel Lives* were a series of short takes on famous
Greeks and Romans, compared and contrasted. Plutarch was a
practical biographer, looking for character traits that would be
useful. "The virtues of these great men serv[e] me as a sort of
looking-glass, in which I may see how to adjust and adorn my
own life." He also wanted to learn from great men's flaws. Marcus
Cato—not Addison's Cato, but an earlier, equally virtuous one—
was, for all his greatness, cheap and cruel, working his slaves
hard, then selling them when they could work no more. "In my
judgment, it marks an over-rigid temper for a man to take the
work out of his servants as out of brute beasts, turning them off
and selling them in their old age, and thinking there ought to be
no further commerce between man and man than whilst there

arises some profit by it." Plutarch was so well known in eighteenth-century America that journalists—who wrote under
pseudonyms—often took their by-lines from him, fully expecting
their readers to recognize the source. Americans might dress like
farmers or, at best, like provincial gentlemen, yet mentally they
wore togas.

Americans were Protestant Christians. When John Jay wrote,
in *Federalist* no. 2, that Americans were "one united people . . .
professing the same religion," he meant Protestantism. The
colony of Maryland had been founded by a Catholic nobleman,
but Anglicans and Methodists overwhelmed the Catholics there.
John Adams never saw a Catholic church until he was almost
thirty-nine years old. "Here is everything," he wrote his wife,
"which can lay hold of the eye, ear and imagination. Everything
which can charm and bewitch the simple and ignorant. I wonder
how Luther ever broke the spell." In 1785, there were only 24,500
Catholics in the United States—less than 1 percent of the population. There was also a handful of Jews, less than one-tenth of
1 percent.

Protestants hardly felt themselves to be "the same religion,"
however. Anglicans, Puritans, Presbyterians, Quakers, and Baptists brought a rich history of mutual dislike to America, and in
most colonies one or the other of the first two sects carved out
privileged positions for themselves. By the eighteenth century
these religious establishments had lost their persecuting force
(though they still retained subsidies). The Puritan theocracy in
New England collapsed not only because Quakers and Anglicans
kept sneaking in, but also because the saints could not establish
who had had a saving experience of conversion, entitling him to
full membership in the community. Two colonies had always
enjoyed complete religious freedom: Pennsylvania, because its

founding Quakers believed in it, and Rhode Island, because Roger Williams thought everyone but him so reprobate that they might as well worship as they pleased. Rhode Island was small and eccentric, so its example counted for little, but Pennsylvania was one of the centers of gravity of the emerging nation. When the founders considered themselves in the world, they defined themselves as Protestants. When they looked at each other, they often disliked what they saw, but they had learned to live with their differences.

The older founders remembered the Great Awakening, a surge of piety in the mid-1730s and early 1740s catalyzed by the charismatic, cross-eyed English evangelist George Whitefield. Whitefield was so peripatetic that he was the first American celebrity: the first person who had been everywhere. (George Washington would be the second.) Franklin, who knew Whitefield well, testified that "every accent, every emphasis, every modulation of the voice, was so perfectly well turned and well placed, that without being interested in the subject, one could not help being pleased with the discourse, a pleasure of much the same kind with that received from an excellent piece of music." Samuel Adams, who heard Whitefield preach when he was a student at Harvard, was deeply interested in Whitefield's subject, and remained a devout churchgoer all his life. Younger founders, having no memory of the Great Awakening, grew up in a cooler temperature of religious practice. One of the attractions of Freemasonry was that it supplied a pseudoreligious pomp and circumstance that American Protestantism lacked.

The founders lived in a world of Protestant Christian landmarks. This shaped their language and their frame of reference. Thomas Paine, one of the very few founders who would become an evangelical unbeliever, began his career by quoting the Bible.

His best-selling *Common Sense* (1775) opens with a discussion of the first book of Samuel, in which the Jews ask Samuel to give them a king. The request displeased Samuel, the Lord, and Paine. "These portions of scripture," Paine wrote, "are direct and positive. They admit of no equivocal construction. That the Almighty hath here entered his protest against monarchical government is true, or the scripture is false." Paine would have second thoughts about scripture. Not his fellow Americans, and not (in public, at any rate) the founders.

What did the founders think about thinking? They had inherited a psychology of the passions, as old as the ancient world. Men were bundles of avarice, anger, pride, gluttony, greed, and libido; the good man called in religion or philosophy to control them. By the eighteenth century, the cataloging of human passions was a fine art. Hamilton in *Federalist* no. 6, recounting the wars and rebellions caused by greed and lust—"Pericles, in compliance with the resentment of a prostitute . . . attacked, vanquished, and destroyed the city of the Samnians"—and Madison in *Federalist* no. 10, enumerating the consequences of ambition and acquisitiveness—"Those who hold and those who are without property have ever formed distinct interests in society"—have the air of professors (Hamilton the flashy showboat, Madison the careful lecturer) teaching a survey course: Passions 101. The young Franklin, who drew up a thirteen-step program for achieving "moral perfection," and the old Franklin, who described his project in his *Autobiography*, packaged the passions into a self-help manual. "I was surprised to find myself so much fuller of faults than I had imagined, but I had the satisfaction of seeing them diminish."

At the end of the seventeenth century, John Locke had proposed a new way to look at the mind. Man was the result of what he perceived through his senses. Locke seemed to show how men learned, and he also suggested that they might not be such dangerous creatures, since the cauldrons of their vices were not self-generated. James Madison gave George Washington a copy of Locke's magnum opus, *Essay on Human Understanding*, and Washington seems to have at least read in the tome, since he spoke of political differences arising from men's different perceptions of their situations. As eighteenth-century men thought more about the doctrine of the senses, it seemed a bit thin. Perhaps there was also an innate moral sense, which supplemented what the mind absorbed through the traditional five. The most famous letter Jefferson ever wrote (famous to us: he would have been mortified to think of strangers reading it) was an outpouring to Maria Cosway, a married woman whom he fell head over heels for in Paris. After she left Paris and him, with Mr. Cosway, Jefferson sent her a long letter in the form of a dialogue between the Head and the Heart, and the most intellectual of the founders came down firmly on the side of the Heart. Had philosophers "ever felt the solid pleasure of one generous spasm of the heart, they would exchange it for all the frigid speculations of their lives."

Passions and senses are fragments of the self. What about the self itself, the Self as a whole, a throbbing, absorbing subject? Rousseau was writing in the eighteenth century, and Wordsworth began writing as the century ended. But both the insight and the narcissism of the romantic age came too late for the founders. It was as remote from them as Marx, Freud, or postmodernism. By missing the romantic revolution, they missed the urge to uncover an authentic inner core, which we, as romanticism's late children, still feel. The founders were always either learning, via their senses, or learning to control themselves. It is perhaps the largest gap between their world and ours.

Money is often the last thing historians or revolutionaries think about; battles, laws, and morals are so much more arresting. The founders are no exception. A century before their revolution, a revolution in modern finance had begun in northwestern Europe, yet only a handful of the founders grasped its significance.

The revolution concerned national debt. Traditionally, debt was a curse, lightened only by taxes, plunder, or theft. In the late seventeenth century, men realized that if debt were paid off to public banks in small amounts at regular intervals over a long period of time, it could be turned into credit. Debt, properly managed, becomes money. Responsible governments could go back to the market repeatedly for new loans at reasonable rates. Holland developed a modern financial system first, followed by Britain. Early in the eighteenth century, France tried following in their footsteps, urged on by a Scottish gambler and financier, John Law. Law's schemes burst, however, ruining him and France. Two of the leading nations of Europe had entered a new financial age; one had pulled back. Would American provincials take the plunge?

Travel, pox, war, factories, news, kings, courts, Greeks, Romans, God, passions, money. These were some of the things the founders knew. How would they use that to help us? Have we left anything out? Read on.

CHAPTER 3

Liberty and Law

AMERICA is about liberty, or it is about nothing. The
founders fought a revolution because Britain was infringing their
rights, and they kept working at their form of government until
they had made one capable of preserving them. In the founders'
minds, government existed to secure "inalienable rights" and "the
blessings of liberty."

The founders did not leave it at that, for they spelled out
which rights and what blessings. The Declaration serenely and
swiftly mentions "life, liberty and the pursuit of happiness." Various specific rights, such as habeus corpus and trial by jury, are
squirreled away in the Constitution. But the country wanted an
even longer list, so the first session of Congress after the Constitution had been ratified produced a bill of rights, which became
the first ten amendments.

The founders also knew that lists of rights were not enough. If the structure of government was not well designed, liberty would be undermined by politicians, overwhelmed by popular opinion, or lost in chaos. Where liberty and law were concerned, the how was as important as the what.

Did the Founders Support the Death Penalty?

The founders lived at a time when people were rethinking the whole question of crime and punishment. In 1763, an Italian journalist, Cesare Beccaria, wrote a book, *On Crimes and Punishments*, which became world famous. Beccaria condemned the savagery and irrationality of eighteenth-century justice. There was much to condemn. One hundred sixty crimes carried the death penalty in Britain. Robert-François Damiens, who tried to stab Louis XV in 1757, was executed after hours of torture, including plucking out his eyes and pouring hot lead into the sockets. Beccaria especially condemned capital punishment. "Is it not absurd, that the laws, which detest and punish homicide, should, in order to prevent murder, publicly commit murder themselves?"—an argument that opponents of capital punishment still make today.

Jefferson read Beccaria, as he read everything else, and in the fall of 1776, when the Virginia Assembly assigned him to a committee to revise the state's penal code, he tried to put Beccaria's ideas into practice, up to a point. Edmund Pendleton, another committee member, cautioned Jefferson against too much reform. Although it was true, Pendleton wrote, that Virginia law punished "too many crimes with death," still, if Jefferson intended "to relax all punishments . . . you must find a new race of men" to inhabit the state. Jefferson had no such intention. He retained capital punishment for murder and treason, and proposed other punishments as replacements for different offenses: rapists would be castrated, and other offenders would be put to hard labor in public. Virginia did not pass Jefferson's proposed reforms, and he had second thoughts about public labor after an unsuccessful trial of it in Pennsylvania. Being "exhibited as a public spectacle, with shaved heads and mean clothing . . . produced in the criminals such a prostration of character, such an abandonment of self-respect," that, instead of reforming them, it "plunged them into the most desperate and hardened depravity." Some fates seemed as bad as, if not worse than, death.

The founders assumed that the national government would not have much to do with crime and punishment. At the Continental Congress, John Witherspoon, Madison's teacher in college, remarked in passing that "nothing relating to individuals could ever come before" them; the states, he assumed, would handle all such matters. Even after the Constitution increased the national government's power, Alexander Hamilton argued that the most power-hungry men would not be tempted to meddle in "the mere domestic police of a state." In the eighteenth century, *police* meant both a community's laws and the police force that enforced them.

Even so, the Bill of Rights discusses capital punishment. The Fifth Amendment assumes that certain criminals will be executed, though it limits the ways in which this may be done. No one may be "deprived of life" without due process of law. There will be no summary judgments—no death warrants by executive order, or punitive special bills in Congress; everyone accused of a capital crime will get a trial. What is more, anyone tried for such crimes must be indicted by a grand jury first (unless he serves in the armed forces during wartime, when swifter justice is practiced). Finally, no one may be put "in jeopardy of life" for the same crime more than once. Prosecutors can't keep trying a man until they hang him.

The Eighth Amendment forbids "cruel and unusual punishment," meaning torture. (Some routine eighteenth-century punishments might strike us as borderline torture today. When John Jay was chief justice, he heard a case of conspiracy to commit mutiny at sea; the defendants were convicted and sentenced to thirty-nine lashes, as well as an hour in the pillory and six months in jail.) Capital punishment was not unusual, and not, by itself, considered unusually cruel.

As commander in chief during the Revolution, Washington did not hesitate to execute, or to threaten it. Major John André, a charming young British spymaster, was caught behind American lines out of uniform and hanged as a spy himself (his agent, Benedict Arnold, got away). As the war wound down, some unpaid, undersupplied American soldiers in New Jersey mutinied. After the mutiny was quelled, two of the ringleaders were shot. Washington was "happy" not to have to execute more, but warned that such "lenity" would not be shown "on any future occasion." After the Battle of Yorktown, but before the peace treaty was signed, pro-British irregulars, based in occupied New York, summarily hanged Captain Josiah Huddy, an American prisoner of war. Washington had a British prisoner of equal rank chosen by lot—Captain Charles Asgill was the unlucky man—and ordered that he be executed, unless the British handed over the irregulars as common criminals. Only an appeal from Asgill's mother to our French allies spared his life.

On other occasions, Washington mitigated the death penalty. When Colonel Henry Lee, a brash cavalry officer, proposed beheading deserters, Washington advised him that that particular form of execution was too drastic. "Examples however severe ought not to be attended with an appearance of inhumanity otherwise they give disgust and may excite resentment rather than terror." After President Washington put down the Whiskey Rebellion, a tax revolt in western Pennsylvania, two of the rebels were convicted of treason and condemned to death; since they were small-fry—the real leaders had fled—Washington pardoned them both. Leadership is an art, and Washington knew there are no hard-and-fast rules. But he never excluded the ultimate penalty.

What Would the Founders Think of Gun Control?

The backstory of the founders' thoughts on the politics of gun ownership begins with the politics of England, one hundred years earlier.

During the reign of James II (1685–1688), Protestant Englishmen feared that they would be disarmed by their Catholic king and bullied by his large professional army and its Catholic officer corps. That is indeed what James planned. His Protestant subjects forestalled him by chasing him from the throne in 1688, with Dutch help. One consequence of the Glorious Revolution was the English Bill of Rights, banning standing armies in England in peacetime and guaranteeing Protestants the right to bear arms "for their defense."

William Blackstone, a mid-eighteenth-century legal commentator, explained the right of "having arms" as a firewall, a "barrier . . . to protect and maintain" other rights when ordinary protections had crumbled. "It is indeed a public allowance, under due restrictions, of the natural right of resistance and self-preservation, when the sanctions of society and laws are found insufficient to restrain the violence of oppression."

The gun provisions of the English Bill of Rights and Blackstone's discussion of them became relevant when the Constitution was being ratified. Patrick Henry and Governor George Clinton of New York feared a stronger federal government. Once the Constitution passed, they offered amendments condemning standing armies, upholding the right to keep and bear arms, and praising militias (ordinary citizens, summoned to fight by their states). "A well regulated Militia composed of the body of the people trained to arms," said the Henryites and Clintonians, "is the proper, natural and safe defence of a free State." After passing through Congress and the massaging hands of James Madison, this became the Second Amendment: "A well regulated Militia, being necessary to the security of a free State, the right of the people to keep and bear Arms shall not be infringed." The slap at standing armies had fallen away, but the militia and the armed citizenry remained, no longer a last resort for Protestants against scheming, aggressive Catholics, but for the states against the federal government (and, in theory, for the people against oppressive government). If guns were illegal, only armies would have guns.

This is where the Second Amendment came from. But several complications must be added. Blackstone is a tricky oracle, for the only absolute in his world is legislative supremacy; what he gives to freedom with the right hand he is always willing to take back with the left, so long as the legislature (or parliament) agrees. The right of "having arms," he acknowledges, is subject to "due restrictions . . . such as are allowed by law."

How can Blackstone's "natural right of resistance" find a place in the Constitution in any case? It is the starting point of the

Declaration of Independence, which opens with a recipe for just revolution. But how can the laws say when they should be overthrown? If things have reached that point, it's time to clear the decks, and not worry about the Bill of Rights.

Was the Second Amendment then a bulwark of liberty, or a pious irrelevance? The framers of the Constitution doubted that any Bill of Rights was necessary, which was why they left it out. Under the Constitution power would derive from the people; how could the people oppress themselves? But Madison became midwife for the Bill of Rights, under pressure from his enemy Patrick Henry, and prodding from his friend Jefferson. Jefferson, the amateur architect, saw a bill of rights as a useful structural prop. "A brace the more will often keep up [a] building which would have fallen" without it, Jefferson wrote him. Some founders believed passionately in the Second Amendment and the other nine. The rest put up with them.

Guns were a fact of the founders' everyday lives. When Israel Putnam was a young farmer in northern Connecticut, he crawled into the den of a wolf who had been preying on his sheep and killed her with a blast of buckshot to the face. The cerebral Jefferson, in one of those sweetly pompous letters of advice that he loved sending his younger relatives, recommended taking walks with a gun. "While this gives moderate exercise to the body, it gives boldness, enterprise and independence to the mind. Games played with a ball . . . are too violent for the body, and stamp no character on the mind." So much for baseball, already being played in early forms. "Let your gun, therefore, be the constant companion of your walks." Even Hamilton, the archetypal urbanite, when he became prosperous enough to build himself a country house in northern Manhattan, would walk around his thirty acres with a dog and a fowling piece.

One special type of gun was known to many of the founders, even though its use was illegal—the dueling pistol. Though Hamilton owned a fowling piece, he did not own dueling pistols, so when Vice President Aaron Burr challenged him to a duel for a political insult in the spring of 1804 he had to borrow a set from his brother-in-law. The pistols were made by the London gunsmith Robert Wogdon, the finest practitioner of his art. They were .544 caliber, meaning their bullets had a diameter of just over half an inch (the 9mm Glock pistols used by the New York Police Department today are about .36 caliber). The barrels were unrifled, but their careful balancing made the pistols accurate at the short distances of dueling. Burr's bullet pierced Hamilton's abdomen, and he died of spinal shock after thirty-six hours of agony. Burr was indicted for murder, but the prosecution lapsed, for no jury would convict a gentleman who had defended his honor.

The founders lived among guns; they would never make them illegal; they would subject them to necessary laws, following Blackstone. And they broke their own laws when honor demanded it.

Would the Founders Be in Favor of Gay Rights?

America was a sexually conservative country. When Gouverneur Morris went to France in 1789 for an extended business trip, he already had a reputation as a ladies' man. He soon found himself in love with the pretty young wife of an elderly count; Morris shared her affections with the father of her child, a Catholic bishop. Despite Morris's worldliness, two Parisian sexual practices—minority tastes, to be sure—shocked him: incest and anal sex (whether between men and women, or men and men). Going in by the back door was as alien even to a randy American as sleeping with your daughter.

Modern Americans hunting for gay founders imagine they have found them in the young officers of Washington's wartime staff. Their letters to each other are indeed full of talk about love, devotion, affection, and the heart. Some of the strongest language passed between Hamilton and Colonel John Laurens. "I wish, my dear Laurens," wrote Hamilton, "it might be in my power . . . to convince you that I love you. . . . You should not have taken advantage of my sensibility to steal into my affections without my consent." Were these twenty-something warriors early gaytriots? We have to be mindful of an eighteenth-century vogue for sensibility, one of the very words Hamilton used. The weepy fiction of Samuel Richardson, and the funny/weepy fiction of Laurence Sterne, had inaugurated a craze for ardent emotions, ardently expressed. You showed the sterling quality of your soul by showing how sensitive—or "sensible"—you were. (Jane Austen would mock the fashion in *Sense and Sensibility*.) There are moments of self-mockery even in Hamilton's effusions. Later in the same letter, he asks Laurens to place an ad in the newspapers for a wife. "I lay most stress upon a good shape. . . . [A] little learning will do. . . . [A]s to fortune, the larger stock of that the better." Hamilton ends by reminding Laurens to tell prospective brides that he is well hung. Twenty-two year olds were as young then as they are now. Hamilton did marry, and had eight children and a sensational (straight) affair.

Baron von Steuben, the brilliant Prussian drillmaster, a lifelong bachelor who surrounded himself with devoted young aides, seems like a better candidate for gayness. The only explicit documentary evidence, however, is ambiguous and, if it is evidence of anything, damning. Gossip in the German courts where Steuben served before coming to America accused him of pedophilia. In 1777 an adviser to the margrave of Brandenburg wrote the prince of Hohenzollern-Hechingen, for whom Steuben had worked, inquiring about reports that he had "taken familiarities with young boys." The adviser described the stories as "vulgar rumors" spread by Steuben's enemies, and wanted to clear his reputation. No reply to the letter survives, though Steuben and the prince later resumed friendly contact. No such accusations were made of Steuben after he came to America.

No one, so far as I know, has noticed William Pierce's description of one of his fellow delegates to the Constitutional Convention. Pierce, who represented Georgia, wrote brief sketches of all the framers, and historians have been mining his portraits ever since. This is how he described sixty-four-year-old Daniel of St. Thomas Jenifer: "Mr. Jenifer is a gentleman of fortune in Maryland. . . . From his long continuance in single life, no doubt but he has made the vow of celibacy. He speaks warmly of the ladies notwithstanding." If this had appeared in *Time* magazine in the 1950s, it would have been a sly outing (compare *confirmed bachelor*), highlighted by the apparent retraction of the second sentence. William Pierce, however, was the opposite of sly (he thought Franklin was a charming old storyteller who wasn't much good at politics, not realizing that storytelling was one of the ways Franklin operated).

There have always been homosexual acts and inclinations. In the face of legal and social condemnation, they flourish only in subcultures. Morris found open homosexuals in France because France had an established aristocracy: a petri dish of wealth, power, and free time that fostered both eccentricity and indulgence. If he had searched the demimondes of the great European cities he lived in, he might have found gay low life. By European standards, America's cities were small and few and its aristocracy provincial. There was no context mitigating the laws, and the laws were blunt. Sodomy was a punishable offense in the Revolutionary army, and Jefferson's reformed criminal code for Virginia would have castrated sodomites as well as rapists. Gays had every reason to keep their practices to themselves.

How Would the Founders Have Fought the War on Drugs?

Every time I talk about George Washington to an audience that is younger than the members of AARP, I get the following question: did Washington grow hemp at Mount Vernon? This irrepressible query is asked by potheads, who know that the answer is yes, and want me to say so publicly. One enthusiast, after the talk, gave me one of those modified dollar bills with "I GREW HEMP" stenciled over Washington's head.

What I tell the hopeful is that Washington indeed grew hemp, but that he grew it for fabric. The master of Mount Vernon was a meticulous farmer, and if he had found an additional intoxicating or medicinal use in any of his crops, he would have recorded it.

Opium was used as a medicine, and was known to be addictive, and cranky founders sometimes accused each other of being in its thrall. John Adams, the crankiest founder, thought Alexander Hamilton relied on opium to get him through long speeches, whereas Gouverneur Morris, the sunniest founder, who nevertheless deeply disliked James Madison, wondered if Madison was an opium addict. Both stories were preposterous.

The drug of choice in late-eighteenth-century America was alcohol. Franklin compiled a list of 128 phrases meaning "He's drunk" (from "He's pissed in the brook" to "He's eaten a toad and a half for breakfast" to "He's mellow"). In a more exalted mood, he cited wine as a mark of divine benevolence. In the miracle at Cana, Jesus converted water into wine (John 2:1–11). "But this conversion," wrote Franklin, "is, through the goodness of God, made every day before our eyes. Behold the rain which descends from heaven upon our vineyards; there it enters the roots of the vines, to be changed into wine; a constant proof that God loves us, and loves to see us happy. The miracle [at Cana] was only performed to hasten the operation." When George Washington first ran for the Virginia House of Burgesses, he wanted the voters who came to the polls to be happy enough to elect him, so he treated them to drinks. (Treating voters was illegal, but universally practiced.) The Washington campaign served 28 gallons of rum, 50 gallons of rum punch, 38 gallons of wine, 46 gallons of beer, and 2 gallons of cider, no doubt hard, for a total of 164 gallons of alcohol. There were 396 voters. Washington won.

Besides the liquor on candidate Washington's bar tab, Americans drank brandy and whiskey, also known as pop-skull. All these libations were unimaginable swill. Beyond the tables of a few epicures—Robert Morris, Thomas Jefferson—good wine was virtually unknown in the country. Yet Americans drank away.

The 1795 frontier uprising known as the Whiskey Rebellion was, despite the comic ring of its name, the most serious domestic violence between the Revolution and the Civil War. The point at issue, however, was not drug use but taxes. Hamilton's financial program required a tax on distilled spirits. Distillers in western Pennsylvania resented paying it, fought gun battles with the local excise collector, and raised a rebel flag. Washington sent an army five times larger than the one he had led across the Delaware before the Battle of Trenton to put the rebellion down, and it melted away.

Before things reached this point, Hamilton defended his excise to Congress. A whiskey tax, he argued, was fair: "There appears to be no article . . . which is an object of more equal consumption throughout the United States." But then he had second thoughts; maybe Pennsylvania frontiersmen did drink more. If so, "it would certainly not be a reason . . . to repeal or lessen a tax, which, by rendering the article dearer, might tend to restrain too free an indulgence of such habits." There, in the midst of a controversy that would lead to rebellion, the founder with the most expansive view of the powers of the federal government staked out the maximum drug war position of his generation: if a tax brings down whiskey consumption, so much the better.

The founders would not have fought a war on drugs.

Did the Founders Practice Censorship?

The founders believed in freedom of the press, but they also didn't like reading lies about themselves in the newspapers.

Benjamin Franklin made a tongue-in-cheek proposal for a "liberty of the Cudgel" to match the liberty of the press. "If an impudent writer attacks your reputation . . . and puts his name to the charge, you may go to him as openly and break his head. If he conceals himself" with a false name, "and you can nevertheless discover who he is, you may in a like manner way lay him in the night." Finally, "if your adversary hire better writers than himself to abuse you the more effectually, you may hire brawny porters" to give him "a more effectual drubbing." Franklin knew what he was criticizing; he had filled his own newspapers with hoaxes and false reports for decades.

In 1798 Congress armed itself with something stronger than a club. The Sedition Act made it a federal crime to print, utter, or publish "any false, scandalous and malicious writing" that defamed the president, Congress, or the government of the United States. One New Jersey man was fined $200 for saying that cannons firing a ceremonial volley in honor of President John Adams should fire through his arse. A dozen other offenders were much more severely punished. Matthew Lyon, a Vermont congressman, was fined $1,000 and sentenced to four winter months in an unheated cell with a smelly latrine for suggesting that Adams be sent to a madhouse. James Callender, an editor in Richmond, Virginia, was fined $250 and jailed for nine months for writing that the Adams administration had been "one continued tempest of malignant passions."

Only eight years before passing the Sedition Act, Congress had passed the First Amendment, which said that Congress "shall make no law . . . infringing the freedom of the press." Some congressmen had supported both measures. How did they square the circle?

The American press was free from prior restraints, such as licensing requirements or submitting stories to censors before publication. But did that guarantee immunity for anything a newspaper then printed? British law had long punished libels (statements that were defamatory or false) and seditious libels (statements that defamed the government). Some of the statements prosecuted under the Sedition Act were not false exactly—Adams's bad days were tempestuous, and he had many—but they were certainly defamatory.

Jefferson and Madison saw the Sedition Act as a federal power grab and an effort to muzzle them and their supporters in the run-up to the election of 1800 (the act was scheduled to sunset in March 1801). The nation agreed, for Jefferson beat John

Adams in 1800, thanks partly to the harshness and pettiness of Sedition Act prosecutions.

Once he was in the White House, Jefferson pardoned Callender and remitted his fine. At the same time, however, he conducted his own backdoor war on press critics whom he considered liars, under the guise of concern for journalistic standards. States had their own laws against seditious libel, and Jefferson wrote friendly governors suggesting that they initiate "a few prosecutions of the most prominent offenders." This "would have a wholesome effect in restoring the integrity of the presses" (Jefferson would muzzle the press to save it).

In this all-too-human political struggle, some of the founders advanced a broader doctrine of freedom of the press. While the Sedition Act was in force, Madison described the "right of freely examining public characters and measures" as "the only effectual guardian of every other right." Without public discussion in the press, political action would become a blind and ineffectual charade. If Sedition Acts had been in force throughout the eighteenth century, Madison pointed out, America might still be "a sickly confederation," or a collection of "miserable colonies."

During the Jefferson administration, Hamilton defended one of the editors that Jefferson's allies found unwholesome. Hamilton, who had himself prosecuted a newspaper that libeled him, now argued that the press had a role in the political system. "We have been careful that when one party comes in, it shall not be able to break down and bear away the other. . . . To watch the progress of such endeavors is the office of a free press. To give us early alarm and put us on our guard against the encroachments of power."

Censorship is ultimately as much about readers as about writers. Can the public be trusted to come to its own conclusions?

President Jefferson wrote the most eloquent defense of the people—they "may safely be trusted to hear everything true and false, and to form a correct judgment between them"—though he did not always practice what he preached.

Would the Founders Permit Assisted Suicide?

Christianity forbids suicide, but the philosophy of the ancient world did not. Founders who felt the call of the latter kept it in mind as an option. In 1813 Jefferson, who had just turned seventy, wrote about the medical uses of various plants. A preparation of Jamestown weed—a.k.a. jimsonweed, an invasive herb whose seeds are a toxic hallucinogen—"brings on the sleep of death as quietly as fatigue does the ordinary sleep. . . . There are ills in life as desperate as intolerable, to which it would be the rational relief, *e.g.*, the inveterate cancer." Jefferson also said that lethal doses of Jamestown weed should be "restrained to self-administration." He would seek death if he felt the need, but he would seek it by himself.

Jefferson died thirteen years after his Jamestown weed letter, age eighty-three, after having struggled successfully to make it to July 4, 1826, the fiftieth anniversary of the Declaration of Independence.

What Would the Founders Say about Stem-Cell Research?

Though cells had been discovered in the late seventeenth century, observed by the first microscopes, stem-cell research was far beyond the horizon of the founders. But they did confront a question of life and death, and the ethics of medical research.

In 1788 John Jay, Robert Livingston, George Clinton, and Baron von Steuben all got sucked into the Doctors' Riot, two days of uproar in New York touched off by obnoxious medical students. One April day a doctor-to-be at New York Hospital (which still exists) was studying anatomy by dissecting a corpse, when he saw a boy peering through the window. He waved a dead arm at the child, saying that it belonged to his mother. The boy told his father, who went to his recently deceased wife's grave and found it empty. Bodies were stolen from graveyards so frequently that those who did it had a name—"resurrection men." An angry crowd broke into the hospital, trashing equipment and retrieving body parts. The next day a mob of five thousand (a fifth of the entire population of the city) ransacked doctors' houses and Columbia College for more cadavers. They ended at the city jail, where the medical community was hiding for safekeeping. The city's elite and a handful of militia tried to turn them back, but were pelted with bricks. Steuben was bloodied, Jay knocked out. The mayor finally ordered the militia to fire, killing three rioters.

Americans understood that doctors needed to "consult . . . dead subjects for the benefit of mankind," as the aggrieved sponsors of one New York cemetery put it. (Benjamin Franklin believed that in only a few centuries the benefits of science would include life spans as long as the patriarchs of the Bible.) But New Yorkers did not want their loved ones to be the guinea pigs. After the Doctors' Riot the state legislature banned the "odious practice" of medical resurrection, offering anatomy students the bodies of executed criminals to learn on instead. Men of science always know what is best for mankind, which tends to be what is best for science. As leaders of society, the founders believed in progress, and as magistrates they did not tolerate disorder, but as politicians they understood that science had to heed public opinion and traditional norms.

What Would the Founders Do about Hurricane Katrina and Other Natural Disasters?

Which branches of government should respond to natural disasters and how? Alexander Hamilton lived through a hurricane, and described it in the media like a youthful Anderson Cooper.

In August 1772, St. Croix in the Virgin Islands was slammed by a hurricane. No one named or rated tropical storms then (the Beaufort scale for measuring wind at sea was not invented until 1806), but this was a bad one. Hamilton, who was fifteen years old at the time, wrote an account that was published in the local newspaper:

> Good God! What horror and destruction. . . . The roaring of the sea and wind, fiery meteors flying about it in the air, the prodigious glare of almost perpetual lightning, the crash of the falling houses, and the ear-piercing shrieks of the distressed, were sufficient to strike astonishment into angels. A great part of the buildings throughout the island are levelled to the ground, almost all the rest very much shattered; several persons killed and numbers utterly ruined; whole families running about the streets, unknowing where to find a place of shelter. . . . In a word, misery, in all its most hideous shapes, spread over the whole face of the country.

In 2004 when St. Croix commemorated the bicentennial of Hamilton's death, that passage was read aloud and compared to the most recent beating the island had taken, Hurricane Georges in 1998.

One of the things the young reporter noted was the authorities' response. The Danish governor-general of the island, Hamilton wrote, "has issued several very salutary and humane regulations, and both in his publick and private measures, has shewn himself *the Man*." Hamilton's italics, Hamilton's capital: even as a teenager, he looked for responsibility in leaders, and equated it with manliness. (Hamilton's father had abandoned his wife and children some time before the hurricane hit, which made young Alexander look all the harder.)

Sixteen years after the hurricane letter, much had changed in Hamilton's life: he had moved to America, fought in a war, become a husband and father, and helped write a constitution. In 1788, he was defending the Constitution in the *Federalist Papers*, and executive responsibility was still on his mind. "Energy in the executive is a leading character in the definition of good government. . . ." he wrote in *Federalist* no. 70. "A feeble executive implies a feeble execution of the government. A feeble execution is but another phrase for a bad execution; and a government ill executed, whatever it may be in theory, must be, in practice, a bad government." Hamilton was not as keen on the checks and balances of the new constitution as his *Federalist* coauthor James Madison; his take-charge personality could make him impatient with such distinctions. But he had signed off on them; as he told the Constitutional Convention in Philadelphia, he would "take any system which promises to save America." He might accept the laws that make local and state authorities the first responders to disaster today. But he would expect mayors, governors, and the president of the United States all to show "energy in the executive."

THE FOUNDERS were more concerned with structure than with specifics. In my lifetime, there have been two amendments to the Constitution. In James Madison's lifetime, there were twelve amendments (the Bill of Rights and two others), besides the Constitution itself, and the American Revolution. The founders destroyed, and built and rebuilt, because they believed that good government was more than a matter of detail. If they got the building right, the furnishings would take care of themselves.

What Did the Founders Mean by Federalism?

The founders were trying to do something that the political writer they most admired told them was impossible—establish a large republic. To do this, they had to resolve the relations between the states and the United States.

Baron de Montesquieu, a liberal Anglophile Frenchman, was one of the founders' intellectual heroes. They cited his 1748 book, *The Spirit of the Laws*, like holy writ, and called him "the celebrated Montesquieu," as if *celebrated* was his first name. This commanding figure had decided that it was "in the nature of a republic to have only a small territory," whereas "a large empire" required "despotic authority in the one who governs." Citizens could mind their own affairs if they lived cheek by jowl; once a country spread beyond the horizon, only one man, untrammeled by checks or limitations, could be in charge.

History seemed to bear Montesquieu out. Most of the republics of the ancient world, and the handful of republics in the eighteenth century (like the Swiss cantons), were scarcely bigger than cities. The great exception was the Roman Republic, which conquered the Mediterranean world, but the exception proved the rule, for Rome had become an empire.

Yet the United States, small in population, was already vast in size. Maine and Georgia were as far apart as London and Belgrade. The first name of the American army was the Continental army. Many of the founders' daydreamed of acquiring Canada and Cuba. Jefferson did manage to reach the Rocky Mountains. How did such a far-flung republic hope to cheat Montesquieu?

The first gambit of the founders was a confederation—assembling a nation from a collection of sovereign states. The Articles of Confederation (approved by Congress in 1777, ratified by 1781) linked the thirteen states in a "league of friendship"—more than an alliance, less than a unification. The states retained "sovereignty, freedom and independence," and "every power, jurisdiction and right" not expressly delegated to Congress.

The national government under the articles was not powerless. It won a war and made a peace. It established the principle that all new states would be equal to the original thirteen, and it was founded on the principle that the Union was "perpetual" (the idea that states had a right to secede is a campfire story of Confederates and their apologists).

The articles failed because state sovereignty was an indigestible obstruction to the day-to-day operations of government. The great weakness of the articles was financial, since Congress could not tax but only ask the states for money. America tried to scrape by on paper money, foreign loans, and kited bills, but by the mid-1780s a deadbeat country had no credit to speak of. The states, left to settle their own debts, had a choice of cheating their creditors or crushing their taxpayers.

The founders who framed the Constitution believed that the national government needed more power. One delegate to the

Constitutional Convention, George Read of Delaware, proposed getting rid of the states entirely. What the Constitution did instead was to create a crosshatch pattern of national and state power; we call the new mixture *federalism*.

The Constitution says nothing about the "sovereignty, freedom and independence" of the states, or of the nation. That is because under federalism, sovereignty is divided. As Madison put it, local authorities are "no more subject, within their respective spheres, to the general authority, than the general authority is subject to them, within its own sphere." "The powers of sovereignty," Hamilton agreed, "are in this country divided between the National and State Governments. . . . Each has sovereign power as to *certain things*, and not as to *other things*." Another way of putting it is that all power comes from the people, sometimes acting in their capacity as New Yorkers or North Carolinians, sometimes in their capacity as Americans.

Since the framers of the Constitution did not intend to be bound by Montesquieu's strictures on size, they had to think of some way of refuting him. Madison managed it by arguing that large republics were not only possible, but actually better than small ones. The diverse interests of a big country guaranteed the liberty of all. "Extend the sphere" of a republic, he wrote, and "you make it less probable that a majority of the whole will have a common motive to invade the rights of other[s]."

The synthesis of federalism left a number of questions undecided. What certain things could states and the national government do, and what other things could they not do? The Constitution lists Congress's powers, forbids others, and forbids still other powers to the states. (To take three examples, Congress can coin money, it can't criminalize actions that have already occurred, and no state can sign treaties). So much is clear. On the other hand, Congress may also pass laws that are "necessary and proper" for carrying out its listed powers. On the third hand, the Ninth and Tenth Amendments reserve all rights and powers that are not listed to the people, and to the states. Between these three points passed lively currents of dispute. Hamilton, as first secretary of the treasury, thought the "necessary and proper" clause allowed Congress (following his advice) to establish a national bank, the better to regulate commerce. Madison feared that such step-by-step reasoning would allow Hamilton (manipulating Congress) to do anything at all. Their disagreements roiled the politics of the 1790s. (One thing the two allies-turned-enemies agreed on was that if Congress wanted to build canals—and both men thought it should—it would need a constitutional amendment allowing it to do so. The "necessary and proper" clause had limits, even for Hamilton.)

Suppose state and national governments disagreed about what their respective spheres of sovereignty were? The "tribunal" resolving such disputes, wrote Madison in 1788, would have to be the "general," or national, government. "Some such tribunal is clearly essential to prevent an appeal to the sword . . . and that it ought to be established under the general rather than under the local governments . . . is a position not likely to be combated." But as time passed, some founders combated it. In 1798, during the storm over the Sedition Act, Virginia resolved that states could "interpose for arresting the progress" of "deliberate, palpable and dangerous exercise[s]" of national power. In 1815, New England, which bitterly opposed the War of 1812, declared that states could "interpose [their] own authority . . . in cases of deliberate, dangerous and palpable infractions of the Constitution." These assertions of old-fashioned state sovereignty depended on whose ox was being gored. Madison, the champion of federalism in 1788, wrote the Virginia Resolutions of 1798, because by then he was in opposition to the Adams administration. But by 1815, he was the president whom New England opposed. Gouverneur Morris was more consistent than Madison, at least as far as constitutional reasoning was concerned. Morris, who hated the War of 1812 as much as any New Englander, did not trifle with questions of state sovereignty. If things were as bad as he thought, then it was time to revolt, plain and simple. "It seems to me," he wrote in 1814, "I was once a member of Congress during a revolutionary war."

The most intelligent founders invented federalism as a flexible system for ruling a large country from the top down and the bottom up simultaneously. The system could not shepherd America through times of internal crisis; by definition, times of crisis are times when systems fail.

What Did the Founders Think of Judicial Review?

Some founders thought judicial review was the last missing piece of the Constitution; others thought it was a blot on free government. The first founder to argue for judicial review was Alexander Hamilton, and he did it before there was a Constitution to which he could appeal.

Joshua Waddington was a British businessman who, during the occupation of New York City in the Revolutionary War, operated a run-down brewery that had been owned by a patriot widow, Elizabeth Rutgers. After the war, New York State passed a law, the Trespass Act, allowing patriots to collect back rent from Tories who had used their property. Mrs. Rutgers demanded 8,000 pounds—more than $300,000 today—and Waddington hired Hamilton to defend him.

In *Rutgers* v. *Waddington*, Hamilton urged the court to ignore the Trespass Act, because the state constitution recognized English common law, which recognized the law of nations and the laws of war, allowing military authorities to regulate property in territory they occupied. Waddington had played by rules that New York was bound to acknowledge. "When statutes contradict . . . maxims of the common law," Hamilton said, "the common law shall be preferred."

The judges came down on neither side, splitting the difference on a technicality and awarding Mrs. Rutgers 791 pounds, but Hamilton had hold of a principle. In the *Federalist Papers,* Hamilton applied his argument for Joshua Waddington to the nation. "Whenever a particular statute contravenes the Constitution it will be the duty of the judicial tribunals to adhere to the latter and to disregard the former."

Hamilton's arguments were taken up in 1803 by Chief Justice John Marshall in *Marbury* v. *Madison.* The case had begun in March 1801, the last days of the Adams administration, when President Adams commissioned several dozen justices of the peace for the District of Columbia. The incoming Jefferson administration, not wanting to be loaded up with Adams's patronage appointments, installed only half of them. William Marbury, who was one of the men who did not get his commission, asked the Supreme Court to order Secretary of State James Madison to appoint him. Marbury appealed to the Judiciary Act of 1789, which gave the Supreme Court the power to issue writs of mandamus (Latin for *we order*) to all federal officeholders.

Chief Justice Marshall, who wrote the opinion, was himself one of Adams's lame-duck appointments, and though he was a cousin of Thomas Jefferson, he detested Jefferson and all his works. But his ruling rose beyond the politics of the moment to claim a more sweeping power. Marshall told Marbury that the Judiciary Act of 1789 was unconstitutional, since the Constitution does not give the Supreme Court the power to issue writs of mandamus. "An act of the legislature repugnant to the constitution is void." When laws were void it was the business of the courts to say so. "It is emphatically the province and duty of the judicial department to say what the law is." Marshall let the Jefferson administration decide the fate of William Marbury—and asserted the courts' power to decide the fate of unconstitutional laws. The Supreme Court never revisited this principle during Marshall's tenure (he died in 1835), but he had laid down a marker.

Jefferson's dislike of Marshall was mutual. He especially disliked Marshall's ability to convert all the men he appointed to the Supreme Court to Marshall's expansive views of judicial power. When he was an old man, Jefferson wrote an antijudicial cri de coeur. He saw judges as political aggressors. "They are in the habit of going out of the question before them, to throw an anchor ahead, and grapple further hold for future advances of power." He also saw them as unchecked, since they served during good behavior, and were removable only by impeachment. "Our Judges are effectually independent of the nation. But this ought not to be. . . . I deem it indispensable to the continuance of this government, that they should be submitted to some practical and impartial control." During his presidency, Jefferson's allies had proposed a variety of constitutional amendments to rein the judiciary in, limiting judges to stated terms or making them removable, not by impeachment, but by simple votes of two-thirds, or even one-half, of Congress. But none of them were ratified.

The founders flatly disagreed on judicial review. But we must also understand what they hoped to achieve by it, or to protect from it. Hamilton and Marshall expected judges to rule as they themselves thought, reasoning from the British common law, and the law of nations. The law they knew was heavy with precedent, and informed by a view of natural right, based on the nature of human beings and society. Jefferson put his faith in the people as lawmakers, at the national, state, or local level, always confident that the people would ultimately choose wisely. Judicial review involves questions of substance as well as structure; it is not only who decides, but why.

CHAPTER 4

God and Man

The founders were not otherworldly men. Their struggles with liberty and law took place in the realm of what the Declaration calls "human events." Yet perhaps human events are not directed solely by human beings.

In the fall of 1778, things were looking up for the American Revolution. France came in on America's side in February; the British evacuated Philadelphia, the capital, in June, and the Battle of Monmouth—nominally a draw, in fact an American victory—soon followed. Congress celebrated by banning plays. "Whereas true religion and good morals are the only solid foundations of public liberty and happiness," Congress asked the states to prohibit "such diversions as are productive of idleness, dissipation, and a general depravity of principles and manners." The French ambassador, observing the peculiar customs of his new allies, explained the maneuver to his government, much as marine generals brief Washington about Shiite clergy in Iraq. "It is the northern members, called the Presbyterian party, that delight in passing moral laws."

Europeans had both rigid religious establishments and a history of recent religious conflict (John Jay's Huguenot grandfather had been expelled from France less than a century earlier). A European would search with eagle eyes for religious politicking in America, sometimes in places where Americans would piously deny—with sincerity, or with cant—that it was going on. Yet there was plenty of religion in America, then as now, and it often impinged on politics. The founders established the regime of religious liberty we now live under, and had many of the same arguments about it that rage today.

Did the Founders Believe We Were One Nation, under God?

The Declaration of Independence made us a nation, and put us under God. It invokes Him four times. In the peroration, Congress added two references to Thomas Jefferson's draft: we relied "on the protection of divine providence," and we appealed "to the supreme judge of the world for the rectitude of our intentions." God was our security and our character reference. Jefferson himself began the Declaration with two more mentions: our independence was an entitlement derived from "the laws of nature and of nature's God," and our rights were the gift of our "Creator." Jefferson wrote another more oblique reference, when discussing the truths that we esteem: he called them "sacred and undeniable." Benjamin Franklin, in the drafting committee, transposed Jefferson's language of devotion to the language of science or geometry, making the truths "self evident."

It would have been astonishing if the Declaration had not mentioned the Almighty. In his old age, Jefferson correctly denied that the Declaration was an anthology of his little thoughts; rather, it was a collective effort, "an expression of the American mind." Like most Americans in the midst of cataclysms, from the Deerfield massacre to Hurricane Katrina, the founders looked to a higher power: they felt moved by it, supported by it, sometimes rebuked and abandoned by it. Two weeks after the Declaration was approved, John Page, a Virginia politician, asked Jefferson, "Do you not think an angel rides in the whirlwind and directs the storm?"

The man who rode in the whirlwind for eight and a half years, directing what he could, enduring what he couldn't, was the American commander in chief, George Washington. This reticent man led the religious life of an English country squire. He served on his parish vestry (Anglican, of course), attended church fairly regularly, never took communion, had no clergy at his deathbed, and kept his lip zipped about the higher things, almost as if it were a matter above his pay grade. He did so with one exception: he spoke constantly of Providence, and its superintending power, in wartime and peacetime. After the Battle of Monmouth (1778) he wrote of "that bountiful Providence which has never failed us." The General Orders after Yorktown (1781) cited the "reiterated and astonishing interpositions of Providence." His first inaugural (1789) dwelled on the "providential agency" at work in the founding—"reflections [which] have forced themselves too strongly on my mind to be suppressed." His decision whether to serve a second term (1792) relied on "the allwise disposer of events [who] has hitherto watched over my steps." Most people who know anything about eighteenth-century religion know, or think they know, that educated men and women believed in a watchmaker God who wound creation up and left it to tick. Washington's watchmaker had his creation on permanent warranty, and was constantly cleaning and tinkering with it.

The founders believed in divine oversight; their ability to acknowledge it was sometimes limited by practical considerations. Late in June 1787, when the Constitutional Convention was mired in its worst deadlock, Benjamin Franklin rose to speak. He quoted Psalm 127. "We have been assured, Sir, in the sacred writings, that 'except the Lord build they labour in vain that build it.' I firmly believe this; and I also believe that without his concurring aid we shall succeed in this political building no better than the builders of Babel." Therefore, Franklin moved that every morning's business begin with a prayer. Roger Sherman and Edmund Randolph agreed with him. But most of the delegates agreed with Hugh Williamson, who pointed out that they had no money to hire clergymen, and with Alexander Hamilton, who argued that such a resolution, coming two months into their work, would look desperate (Hamilton is also supposed to have joked that they should not call in foreign aid). The convention declined to vote on Franklin's motion. The Constitution, when finally written, made no mention of God, and why should it? It is a structure; the statement of principles was in the Declaration.

Did the Founders Think America Was a Christian Nation?

In 1797, the Senate considered a treaty, negotiated the previous year, with the bashaw of Tripoli. The United States agreed to give him cash and presents, and declared, in one clause, that America bore "no character of enmity against the laws, religion, or tranquility of Musselmens," for it was "not, in any sense, founded on the Christian religion." Tripoli and the countries of North Africa ran a naval protection racket, extorting ransoms for captives they seized, or selling their good behavior, in treaties such as this one. North African slavery was horrible, and since the United States could not protect its shipping or its citizens, it found it prudent to pay in advance. Tripoli's true religion was thievery, but the clause on Christianity and Islam was designed to remove any pretext for trouble. The Senate passed the treaty unanimously, and President Adams signed it three days later. When honor yields to necessity, there is no point quibbling over details. (Four years later the bashaw upped his price and declared war, forcing us to deal with him differently.)

In fact, there was no cause to quibble with the bashaw about creeds. The United States was not founded on the Christian religion. The First Amendment, forbidding a national religious establishment, had been ratified in 1791. The year before, President Washington wrote the congregation of Touro Synagogue in Newport that America did not practice "toleration": it was not "by the indulgence of one class of people, that another enjoyed the exercise of their inherent natural rights. . . . All possess alike liberty of conscience and immunities of citizenship." In 1793, he wrote the Swedenborgian New Church in Baltimore "that every person may here worship God according to the dictates of his own heart." That amendment and these statements are a better guide to the founders' views than a treaty with pirates.

Washington had invoked Christ in one critical public statement, his 1783 circular to the states as the Revolution was winding down. This, as far as Washington knew at the time, was his farewell address, his last significant official communication with the state governments and the people of America. He ended it with a prayer that God (a more particular name than Providence) would "dispose us all, to do justice, to love mercy, and to demean [conduct] ourselves with that charity, humility and pacific temper of mind, which were the characteristicks of the divine author of our blessed religion, and without an humble imitation of whose example in these things, we can never hope to be a happy nation." The Touro Synagogue would be pleased that he quoted Micah 6:8 on the importance of justice and mercy. But neither they nor any Musselmens who happened to be in America would consider Jesus Christ the author of their religions. Washington was not asking Americans to think of Jesus in a religious context, however—as Savior, or Son of God. He was asking them to imitate Jesus' qualities—charity, humility, peacefulness. Washington had seen little enough of "pacific temper" during the war, and he would see little more when he came back into public life as president. But some sufficient residue had to exist, or the country would fly apart. Whatever Washington believed about Christ, the Christ of his statement is a political figure, the model citizen.

What Role Did the Founders Believe That Religion Should Play in Public Life?

In March 1790, one month before he died, Benjamin Franklin answered a letter from the Reverend Ezra Stiles, a Congregationalist minister and president of Yale College. Stiles wanted to know what Franklin believed. Franklin answered that this was the first time anyone had ever asked him (clearly, he did not believe in the Ninth Commandment), then stated his creed. It was essentially Unitarian: God rules the world, the best way to serve him is by serving mankind, and Jesus was a great moral teacher. Franklin doubted Jesus' divinity, but would not worry about the matter now, "when I expect soon an opportunity of knowing the truth with less trouble." If believing in Jesus' divinity encouraged people to follow his teachings, that was probably a good thing. Franklin ended by asking Stiles to keep his letter confidential. "All sects here [in Philadelphia] have experienced my good will in assisting them with subscriptions for building their new places of worship; and, as I have never [publicly] opposed any of their doctrines, I hope to go out of the world in peace with them all." Franklin believed that religion was good for the public; if the public thought he was religious, that was good for Franklin.

If the founders did not make America a Christian nation, many of them thought it should be a religious nation. In their view religions sustained the civic culture of the state. Franklin said as much in his letter to Stiles; George Washington said it quite directly in his actual Farewell Address, printed in the newspapers in 1796 as his last term was ending. "Of all the dispositions and habits which lead to political prosperity," Washington wrote, "religion and morality are indispensable supports." He also called them "pillars of human happiness" and "props of the duties of men and citizens." He gave an example: "Where is the security for property, for reputation, for life, if the sense of religious obligation desert the oaths" taken in court? (Was Washington right? Two hundred years later, the nation would be convulsed because President Clinton lied under oath, yet Clinton was a religious man.) Philosophy could not do the job of propping, pillaring, and supporting alone. "Reason and experience both forbid us to expect that national morality can prevail in exclusion of religious principle."

The background of these concerns was the French Revolution, by then in its eighth year. Its enemies, who by 1796 included Washington, often argued that the revolution threatened the political and moral fabric of the world. Washington wanted to shore up America. He proposed no government action; given his political principles, how could he? He called for intellectual, and individual, vigilance. What friend of "free government," he asked, "can look with indifference upon attempts to shake the foundation . . . ?"

Other founders thought free government was threatened by religion, not revolution. Thomas Jefferson was an enthusiastic supporter of the French Revolution because he believed, as he wrote George Wythe, that France had been "loaded with misery, by kings, nobles, and priests, and by them alone." France's clerical establishment had been as crushing as its political one. America was fortunate not to have such a thing, but politicized orthodoxy was a threat even here. That, Jefferson believed, was why the principles of liberty had to be entrenched in law, and publicly honored. During his first term as president, he sent a letter to supporters in Danbury, Connecticut, in which he admitted religious feelings—for the First Amendment. "I contemplate with sovereign reverence that act of the whole American people." The First Amendment, he explained, after quoting it, "buil[t] a wall of separation between church and state." The wall of separation had holes in it, as Jefferson knew, for the First Amendment allowed states to maintain religious establishments, and several, including Connecticut, did so; the supporters, to whom he was writing, were a group of Baptists who chafed at their minority position in a Congregationalist state. But Jefferson hoped to see "the progress of those sentiments which tend to restore to man all his natural rights."

Washington and Jefferson were both amateur architects, whose houses—Mount Vernon and Monticello—are American masterpieces. Building metaphors came naturally to them. But when they looked to religion, from the point of view of freedom, Washington thought of pillars, Jefferson of walls.

Were There Any Evangelicals or Atheists among the Founders?

The religion of the founders, as Washington and Franklin expressed it, can seem cool to us. Franklin had known George Whitefield, the greatest evangelist of the eighteenth century, printing his sermons and feeling the force of his preaching. Yet Franklin was not converted, settling—or settling back—into a rather distant Unitarianism. Washington, though he believed in a Providence that ruled the world and the battlefield, was reticent about doctrine. His only references to an afterlife appear in letters written after the death of his mother (she was now, he hoped, in "a happier place"). At the same time, the unbelief of the founders seems strangely pious. Historian Joseph Ellis, in *American Sphinx*, wrote that "in modern day parlance," Jefferson "was a secular humanist." But that gives a wrong impression. What modern-day atheist, in the mold of Christopher Hitchens, would pore over the Gospels, as Jefferson did, trying to sift Jesus' authentic from his spurious sayings? "I have performed this operation for my own use," Jefferson informed John Adams in 1814. "The matter which is evidently his"—forty-six pages—"is as easily distinguishable as diamonds in a dunghill." Christianity might be politically dangerous, and its doctrines absurd, but its founder preached "the most sublime and benevolent code of morals which has ever been offered to man." Secular humanists should be made of sterner stuff.

Where is the buzz of American religion, its zealous masses of faithful, its strident minority of carpers? It was there too, among the founders. Samuel Adams was a combination of Puritan throwback and modern believer, touched by the religious revival of the Great Awakening. Like Franklin, he had heard Whitefield preach, but unlike Franklin, he was moved by what he heard. In later life he told his relations that "religion in a family is at once its brightest ornament, and its best security." He thought religion was also the best security for society. After the British evacuated Boston in March 1776, he looked forward to "the happy opportunity of re-establishing ancient principles and purity of manners." When Bostonians used their freedom instead to dance, play cards, and watch plays, he feared the worst.

> It was asked in the reign of Charles the Second of England, How shall we turn the minds of the people from an attention to their liberties? The answer was, By making them extravagant, luxurious and effeminate. . . . I love the people of Boston. I once thought that city would be the *Christian Sparta*. But alas! Will men never be free? They will be free no longer than while they remain virtuous.

Thomas Paine attended Methodist services as a young man, and his early American polemics quote the Bible. But by the time he reached *The Age of Reason* (1794–1795), he was assailing organized religion, especially Christianity.

> What is it the bible [Paine's lowercase] teaches us? Rapine, cruelty, and murder. What is it the testament teaches us? To believe that the Almighty committed debauchery with a woman engaged to be married. . . . Of all the systems of religion that ever were invented, there is none more derogatory to

the Almighty, more unedifying to man, more repugnant to reason, and more contradictory in itself than this thing called Christianity.

Unlike Jefferson, Paine found Jesus' moral teachings neither sublime nor benevolent: turning the other cheek meant "sinking man into a spaniel."

Samuel Adams and Paine went head-to-head over religion in 1803. Adams started it, writing a letter to Paine praising him as "a warm friend to liberty," but hammering the "defence of infidelity" he had made in *The Age of Reason*. "Do you think that your pen . . . can unchristianize the mass of our citizens, or have you hopes of converting a few of them to assist you in so bad a cause?" Paine's answer reaffirmed his faith in God (the deist one), downplayed somewhat his anti-Christianity, and tried to patch things up. "If I do not believe as you believe, it proves that you do not believe as I believe, and this is all that it proves."

It was an uncharacteristically mild performance on Paine's part, and there was a reason for this. When Paine was involved in controversy, he tended to pull rank as a revolutionary. Paine was the second most radical man in America, the most blazing writer, and the earliest advocate of independence. "Common Sense" called for a break with Britain in February 1776, five months before Congress got around to it. But he was not the most radical man; that was Samuel Adams. Paine urged men to fight for their rights; Adams sent mobs into the streets (he did it as early as 1765). Paine mocked monarchy and its agents; Adams had their houses burned down. Paine was theory and glorious rhetoric; Adams was action. Paine defied tyranny; Adams broke laws. Beside Sam Adams even Tom Paine felt a bit like a spaniel.

What Would the Founders Think of Masonry?

This question will baffle most of the readers of this book, and in-flame the rest. Among the baffled will be all the historians, who equate Masonry with the antics of Ralph Kramden's Raccoon Lodge, and therefore assume that it is beneath their professional notice. (Yet they sit through faculty meetings.) In my experience as a speaker, however, the second most commonly asked question about George Washington is, *Was he a Mason?* (For no. 1, see "Would the Founders Fight the War on Drugs?" above.) Some of the questioners are Masons who know the answer is yes, and are fishing for a compliment. The rest are anti-Masons, who don't know the answer, but deeply hope it's no. Masonry is a minority interest, but those who care about it care passionately.

Modern Freemasonry began in 1717 in Britain, when gentle-men took over a craft guild and made it a fraternal organization of their own. Their creed was standard enlightenment fare—benevolence, brotherhood, belief in God without the rites and controversies of the churches. In place of the baggage of religion, they unpacked their own baggage of myths and theatrics that they claimed went back to the reign of King Solomon. Masonry spread like wildfire through the English-speaking world and Eu-rope. The *Constitutions* of Masonry were first published in North America in 1734, by Benjamin Franklin. Washington became a Mason in his early twenties; when he laid the cornerstone of the Capitol in 1793, he wore his Masonic apron. Lafayette belonged to a French lodge.

Masonry soon became politicized in Europe, where church and state were fused, and any brand-new quasi-religious body would be by definition rebellious, like the Falun Gong in commu-nist China today. Masonry did not become political in America until the 1820s, when William Morgan, a renegade Mason who threatened to expose the order, vanished in upstate New York. His disappearance was slackly investigated, and people rushed to the conclusion that there had been a murder and a cover-up. For a few years, what happened to Morgan was the hot topic of the tinfoil-hat brigade, just as what happened to Vince Foster was in the 1990s. A new political party was formed to combat Masonry; it held the first political convention in American history in 1831. The organizers invited one of the last living founders, Chief Justice John Marshall, to attend. Though Marshall had been a Mason since the Revolution, the Morgan affair had changed his opinion of Masonry, from a "harmless plaything" to an institution "capable of producing much evil." Marshall came for one day, but was not impressed by what he saw, for he refused to let his name be placed in nomination. The Anti-Masons turned to their B-list, carried only one state, and fizzled away.

Masonry flourished in eighteenth-century America because, in an austere religious environment, it gave ritual expression to universal ideals. Calvinists and Quakers, Baptists and Methodists worshiped simply on principle; Episcopalians had not yet experienced the Anglo-Catholic revival. Catholics, with their candles and incense, were less than 1 percent of the population. Masons talked sense and put on a good show. Soon enough, though, Masons took their innovations too far. They multiplied degrees and ceremonies, exciting the revulsion of people like William Morgan. (Some evangelicals and traditionalist Catholics, alert for signs of blasphemy, share that revulsion today—hence my questioners.) Masonry in 1831, if not evil, was not the organization Washington, Franklin, and young John Marshall had joined.

Now, when the country is full of fraternal organizations and all of them are losing members, Masonry has changed again. It is not unique, and it is graying. The founders would probably agree, with most of you, that the question is no longer important.

Should Religion Be in Politics?

The founders disagreed about whether religion should be in public life, supporting free government or, at the state level, being supported by it. But they all agreed, as candidates and party leaders, that religion should be in politics.

As Thomas Jefferson moved closer to the center of power, his enemies rang the changes on his unorthodoxy. He was supposed to have acquired his sinister beliefs while he was minister to France (1785–1789), though John Adams had been in and out of France from 1778 to 1783, and he seemed to have escaped the contagion. Jefferson, wrote Alexander Hamilton, "drank deeply of the French Philosophy, in religion, in science, in politics." During the election of 1800, Fisher Ames wondered why Federalist newspapers didn't hammer harder at Jefferson's "irreligion" and "wild philosophy." Hamilton tried, writing his old coauthor John Jay that Jefferson was "an *Atheist* in religion and a *Fanatic* in politics." The two naturally went together. Samuel Adams's clash with Thomas Paine over religion was in part an effort by both men to defend Jefferson against such attacks. "Our friend, the present President of the United States," Adams wrote, "has been calumniated for his liberal sentiments by men who have attributed that liberality to a latent design to promote the cause of infidelity." This slander was "without a shadow of proof." Paine responded mildly, not just to protect himself from Adams, but also to protect Jefferson by lowering the temperature of the argument. No wonder Jefferson had a pious dread of politicized religion and religious politicking. The "irritable tribe of priests,"

Jefferson wrote Benjamin Rush, feared his election, and they were right to do so, "for I have sworn upon the altar of God eternal hostility against every form of tyranny over the mind of man."

Except that Jefferson engaged in religious politicking himself. The man who was shocked at the religious attacks of his enemies welcomed and cultivated religious allies. The Baptists of Danbury, Connecticut, recipients of his "wall of separation" letter, were outsiders in Federalist Connecticut. Jefferson, who could not carry Connecticut in three presidential campaigns, wished the Baptists well out of principle: the principle of religious liberty, and the ancient political principle that the enemy of my enemy is my friend. Jefferson and James Madison had won the friendship of Virginia's Baptists in the same way, by successfully disestablishing the state's Anglicans. Jefferson weighed the political sentiments of Virginia's churches like Karl Rove.

> I must explain to you the state of religious parties with us. One third of our state is Baptist, one third Methodist, and of the remaining third two parts may be Presbyterian and one part Anglican. The Baptists are sound republicans and zealous supporters of their government. The Methodists are republican mostly. . . . The Presbyterian clergy alone (not their followers) remain bitterly federal and malcontent with their government. They are violent, ambitious of power, and intolerant in politics as in religion.

Intolerant, anyway, of Thomas Jefferson.

The founders began meddling with religion as they began to meddle with partisanship. Madison expressed their common view, in *Federalist* no. 10, that political parties and interest groups were bad things, "factions": dedicated to their own, not the common, good; self-interested, not public spirited. Yet he concluded that there were only two ways to check their influence: either by choking off freedom (a monstrous option) or by pulling as many factions as possible into the national arena, where they would act as watchdogs on each other. Though Madison's father was a bishop and his youthful mentor, James Witherspoon, was a minister, he had no adult interest in religion. His political sophistication allowed him to foresee, if only dimly, that he and the other founders would be bringing religion into politics.

CHAPTER 5

Money and Business

*T*HE FOUNDERS' religious beliefs could touch the core of their lives, just as ours can. But much of ordinary life is consumed with work—with getting and spending—and countries, no less than people, need to make money. How should Americans live? How much of their livelihood can a government legitimately take in taxes? The founders discussed these questions passionately, and often intelligently.

One of the founders was a businessman in the modern tycoon sense. Robert Morris's ventures stretched from China to France. On the eve of the Battle of Princeton, he met the American army's payroll out of his own pocket. He had hopes of becoming one of the major bankers in Europe, before he ended up in debtors' prison. But below his lonely eminence in high-rolling, even founders who were farmers had to sell their crops, buy their necessities, and show a little creativity on the side. Thomas Jefferson ran a successful nail-making business at Monticello (which didn't prevent him from joining Morris in bankruptcy).

From time to time, Morris, Jefferson, and other founders looked up from their day jobs to consider the economy as a whole, bringing prejudice, ignorance, ideology, experience, and brilliance to questions of private and public finance.

Were the Founders Tax Revolutionaries?

Spasms of resistance to high taxes are called "tax revolts." The American Revolution was a tax revolt too, though it was a matter of right rather than tax rates. Because the colonists taxed themselves in their own legislatures, they believed that Parliament, to which they elected no members, could not squeeze extra taxes from them. "I think the Parliament of Great Britain," George Washington wrote one of his in-laws in 1774, "hath no more right to put their hands into my pocket, without my consent, than I have to put my hands into your's, for money." Samuel Johnson, the English journalist, told the Yankees (in his pamphlet *Taxation No Tyranny*) they had no business complaining, since most Englishmen cast no votes in parliamentary elections either. But the Americans were not persuaded.

The first American constitution, the Articles of Confederation, confirmed the former colonies, now states, in their taxing powers, and put no effective national taxing power over them. Congress could ask the states for money, which paid or not as they liked. Robert Morris, serving as superintendent of finance, said that getting money out of the states was "like preaching to the dead." The dead were happy with the arrangement; Rhode

Island resolved that the power to withhold revenue was "the most precious jewel of sovereignty."

The Constitution pocketed the precious jewel of state sovereignty by giving the federal government power to levy its own taxes. Soon the founders were disagreeing over how heavy federal taxes should be. The Washington and Adams administrations, guided by the policies of Alexander Hamilton, wanted to pay America's creditors, without extinguishing its debts altogether. Once American IOUs were paying dividends, they would acquire value, and add liquidity to the economy: as Hamilton put it, when "the national debt is properly funded . . . it answers most of the purposes of money." As the international scene darkened in the 1790s, President Adams looked to military preparedness as a safeguard. Congress voted funds for an army, which Adams did not particularly want, and for a navy, which he wanted very much. All these expenditures—debt service, defense spending—required taxes, first on luxuries like coffee, tea, and liquor, then on necessities like salt.

Thomas Jefferson, and his right-hand man, James Madison, came to office vowing to cut taxes and pay off the national debt. They would cut spending and get the debt monkey off the nation's back. Albert Gallatin, a brilliant Swiss immigrant who would serve both men as treasury secretary, calculated in 1801 that he could pay off the national debt with low taxes in sixteen years. Gallatin made progress, though he had to digest unexpected expenses, such as fighting pirates in North Africa and buying Louisiana. Hardest to bear was the wastefulness of some of President Madison's nominal supporters. "I cannot consent," Gallatin complained, to become "a seeker of resources for the purpose of supporting useless baubles." The War of 1812 consumed all the accumulated savings of the Jeffersonians, and threw the government back into debt and taxes once more.

Once the founders had won independence, they did not tolerate tax revolts except in the modern sense of quarrels over tax rates. The Whiskey Rebels, who refused to pay the excise on distilled spirits in 1794, thought they were invoking the spirit of '76. But President Washington thought they were feeding the spirit of anarchy. "If the laws are to be so trampled upon, with impunity, and a minority . . . is to dictate to the majority there is an end put, at one stroke, to republican government." If the people's representatives voted a tax, then the people would have to pay it, until they chose new representatives. Jefferson called his low-tax administration a second American revolution, but he had won it at the ballot box.

Would the Founders Be in Favor of Luxury Taxes?

In January 1788, Alexander Hamilton complained that there was a "real scarcity" of "productive sources of revenue" in the United States. He was thinking of the state of an economy that had little manufacturing, some trade, and a few cash crops. But the not-yet-ratified Constitution, which he had helped frame the year before, would limit potential revenue still further by prohibiting certain kinds of federal taxes. There could be no taxes on exports (Article 1, Section 9)—a nonnegotiable demand of the southern states, which grew the most valuable export crops (tobacco, rice, indigo). "Direct" taxes had to be apportioned among the states according to population (Article 1, Section 9). This meant that any national property or income tax would in fact have only an indirect relation to the actual value of what was being taxed: large states would always have to pay more than small ones, no matter how rich or poor they were. The only direct tax that could be completely equitable—a poll, or head, tax, levied on the population itself—had a kink built into it: since each slave would be counted (Article 1, Section 2) as three-fifths of a person, states with few or no slaves would be taxed at a disproportionately high rate. The federal government would have to be desperate indeed to resort to such measures (Hamilton himself said he disliked poll taxes).

What did that leave, once the Constitution was ratified later in 1788 and Hamilton became first treasury secretary the following year? Duties (taxes on imports) and excises (taxes on production, sale, and consumption). In his first major report to Congress (*Report on Public Credit,* 1790) Hamilton singled out three imports (wine, coffee, tea) and one homemade product (distilled spirits). He saw taxes on all these items as luxury taxes, even sin taxes: "The consumption of ardent spirits particularly . . . is carried to an extreme, which is truly to be regretted."

In 1794, Hamilton proposed another luxury tax, $16—about $250, adjusted for inflation—on every carriage. (Today we might tax Hummers or Gulfstreams, and hit them harder.) This provoked howls of protest, and a lawsuit, from Virginia. The term *limousine liberals* was coined in 1969 by Mario Procaccino, a politician who didn't have a limousine. In 1794 Virginia was full of carriage Republicans—gentleman planters who disliked Hamilton and all his works. Their suit (*Hylton* v. *United States*), which came before the Supreme Court in 1796, argued that the carriage tax was a direct tax on property.

Hamilton, who had by then gone back to his private career as a lawyer, defended his own tax. He could "wring emotion" from tax law, wrote biographer John C. Miller, the way other lawyers do from "widows and orphans." Hamilton argued that carriages were luxuries. "I once had a carriage myself, and found it convenient to dispense with it. But my happiness is not in the least diminished!" The Court ruled that since there was no way to apportion a carriage tax equitably—how would a state in which there were no carriages pay it?—it was indeed an excise.

One reason Hamilton relied on luxury taxes was to "lessen the necessity" of direct ones. But in 1798, Congress, fearing a war with France, decided to raise $2 million from direct taxes on land, property, and slaves. Hamilton, who had come out of retirement to serve in the newly expanded army, heartily approved of the measure. The property assessments were so onerous, however, that German-speaking farmers in eastern Pennsylvania chased off a U.S. marshal who had come to enforce them. It was the Whiskey Rebellion, the second time as farce. There was no fighting, no deaths; the Germans intended no rebellion. President Adams ordered out the military nevertheless ("Whenever the government appears in arms," wrote Hamilton approvingly from the sidelines, "it ought to appear like a *Hercules*"). The ringleaders were arrested and convicted, three of them sentenced to death, then belatedly pardoned. The Federalists never carried Pennsylvania again.

Hamilton had been right to be wary of direct taxes.

Would the Founders Save the Family Farm?

The most rapturous praise of farms and farmers was written by the master of Monticello, Thomas Jefferson, in his *Notes on Virginia*. "Those who labor in the earth are the chosen people of God." How did Jefferson know this? Because farmers never show "corruption of morals." They look "up to heaven, to their own soil and industry . . . for their subsistence," and therefore stand erect in the world, whereas city dwellers who depend on the "caprice of customers" live in a perpetual servile crouch. Freedom can best be enjoyed by freemen, and only farmers are truly free.

Jefferson wrote *Notes on Virginia* to answer the curiosity of a French friend about his homeland. He laid it on a bit thick for a foreign audience, singling out qualities that would pique the interest of jaded sophisticates. But James Madison wrote essentially the same thing for a Philadelphia newspaper: "The life of the husbandman is pre-eminently suited to the comfort and happiness of the individual. . . . 'Tis not the country that peoples either the Bridewells [a London prison] or the Bedlams [a London madhouse]." Madison drew the same political conclusion from his analysis of country life that Jefferson did: "Citizens who provide at once their own food and their own raiment . . . are the best basis of public liberty, and the strongest bulwark of public safety."

Jefferson, Madison, and many other founders, north and south, owned large farms, which didn't mean they worked on them personally. Founders who did had somewhat different views of rural life. When John Adams was a boy he told his father that he did not want to go to school. When the elder Adams asked John what he expected to do with his life, John said he would be a farmer, like his father. John's father decided to show him what farming was like, waking him at dawn to cut thatch. After a long, muddy day, John insisted that he liked farming very well. "Ay, but I don't like it so well," his father said, "so you shall go to school." Adams went to school, Harvard, and the White House, though he kept a farm in his hometown and worked on it whenever he was able to live there.

Alexander Hamilton grew up in the most profitable agricultural territory in the world, the sugar islands of the Caribbean (in 1773, Jamaica's exports to Britain were worth five times the exports of all the thirteen colonies). Caribbean sugar production was also the most inhumane agriculture in the world, performed by armies of wretched slaves, often for the benefit of absentee owners. But the ports of the Caribbean were also hubs of international trade, which opened young Hamilton's eyes to the possibilities of a more variegated economy. He unfolded his vision in his 1791 *Report on Manufactures*, a blunt answer to the agrarian ideal. Economic diversity, Hamilton wrote, made a country stronger, not weaker. "The spirit of enterprise . . . must be less in a nation of mere cultivators, than in a nation of cultivators and merchants; less in a nation of cultivators and merchants, than in a nation of cultivators, artificers and merchants." Economic diversity also made people better by developing their potential. "When all the different kinds of industry obtain in a community, each individual can find his proper element, and can call into activity the whole vigor of his nature."

The argument between manufactures and farming was essentially an old argument between luxury and the simple life. Which was better: Athens or Sparta? Imperial Rome or republican Rome? Simple life has a long literary tradition celebrating it, running back to Horace, Virgil, and Hesiod. In the eighteenth century David Hume, with his delight in overturning old pieties, had come down firmly on the side of luxury, and Gouverneur Morris, footloose in Europe after serving as ambassador to France, found himself thinking a very Humean thought. Morris was shocked by the crude hovels of German peasants. How to improve their condition? His remedy was to tax them. Taxes "would draw forth more efforts of body and mind." If the revenues were spent on manufactures, there would be "new objects of desire." "Avarice and sensuality" would then create national wealth, which would become "the footstool of freedom." Men only become free after they work their way to a high level of civilization. This was vintage Morris: a striking idea phrased in the most offensive possible way. He kept this thought to his diary.

Hamilton wanted to jump-start American manufacturing by paying subsidies to infant industries, and by offering rewards to inventors and talented immigrants. He also encouraged a New Jersey corporation, the Society for the Establishment of Useful Manufactures (SEUM), to use the falls of the Passaic River—a beauty spot where he and Washington had picnicked after the Battle of Monmouth—as a power source for factories. Hamilton's plans all failed. Congress would not vote money for bounties or rewards, and the SEUM went bust when the president of the board of directors raided the funds to play in the stock market. Ironically, it was President Jefferson who boosted American manufacturing when he decided, for foreign policy reasons, to forbid trade with Britain and France in 1807 (the embargo lasted a year). President Madison boosted manufacturing yet more when the War of 1812 cut off trade again. Jefferson, in retirement at Monticello, told a correspondent in 1813 that he had thirty-five spindles, a hand-carding machine, and looms with flying shuttles for making cloth. "I have not formerly been an advocate for great manufactories. . . . But other considerations [that is, the destruction of trade] have settled my doubts."

Farming now accounts for 2 percent of America's gross domestic product. The question of profitability has been answered: the spirit of enterprise is greater in a mixed economy. But the psychological question the founders addressed is still relevant: What is the best source for habits of freedom? The experience of independence that farmers enjoy (and if farms dwindle, must there be some functional equivalent)? Or personal development, fostered by the sophistication of daily life, and by education?

Would the Founders Be in Favor of Outsourcing?

The goods and services the founders used were often more local than ours. The Bank of North America did not have clerks in India, nor did carriage makers have their wheels made in Mexico. Even so, material, products, and people crossed the globe, and so the founders had to ask themselves what should be made at home, or fetched from abroad.

Thomas Jefferson, in some moods, was not reluctant to see the high-tech jobs of his day done elsewhere. He believed it was a matter of political hygiene. Better, he wrote in *Notes on Virginia*, to export food and raw materials to workers in Europe, and then import their products, than to import workers to the food and raw materials here, because the workers would bring "their manners and principles" with them—bad manners and bad principles, it was needless to add.

But there were economic reasons behind Jefferson's desire to leave skilled workers in Europe, which had recently been formulated by the Scottish professor Adam Smith. In *The Wealth of Nations* (1776) Smith argued that if other countries can make something more cheaply than yours, then let them. "The tailor does not attempt to make his own shoes, but buys them of the shoemaker. The shoemaker does not attempt to make his own clothes, but employs a tailor. . . . What is prudence in the conduct of every private family, can scarce be folly in that of a great kingdom."

All the founders were familiar with Smith, but they used him as they saw fit. "The principles of the book are excellent," wrote Representative Fisher Ames, "but the application of them to America requires caution. . . . [C]ommerce and manufactures merit legislative interference in this country much more than would be proper in England." Ames was writing in the spring of 1789, when Congress was debating the first tariff bill under the new Constitution. Ames's colleague in the House, James Madison, proposed a 5 percent duty on all imports, for the purpose of raising revenue, and suggested that Congress could raise higher duties on individual items. Congress liked the idea of massaging tariffs. South Carolina wanted a duty on hemp. Massachusetts wanted a low duty on molasses, since that was the primary ingredient of rum, a Massachusetts product. Pennsylvania senator Robert Morris proposed high duties on "a long list" of iron products: scythes, sickles, axes, spades, shovels, locks, hinges, and plow irons. One of his colleagues was "surprised" that Morris said nothing about leather, canes, walking sticks, whips, clothes, brushes, jewelry, or tableware. Other senators said it for him.

Congress would not heed Alexander Hamilton's proposals for an ambitious scheme of promoting new American manufacturing, but it was eager to protect the businesses that America already had. Years later Madison acknowledged Congress's right to impose protective tariffs, and pointed to the first session of Congress as proof. Many of the members had either helped write the Constitution or debated it during their state-ratifying conventions (Madison had done both), yet "it does not appear from the printed proceedings . . . that the power was denied by any of them." Politicians deciding these questions in the future would have to be guided, as those in 1789 had been, by the opinions of their constituents—"whose right and duty it is," Madison concluded, "to bring their measures to the test of justice and of the general good."

What Was Welfare as the Founders Knew It?

As political theorists, the founders thought of poor people as an interest group that had to be balanced against other interest groups. If any achieved dominance, tyranny might result. "In every country where industry is encouraged," said Alexander Hamilton at the Constitutional Convention, expressing the conventional (and Conventional) wisdom, "there will be a division . . . into the few [the rich] and the many [the poor]. . . . Give all power to the many, they will oppress the few. Give all power to the few, they will oppress the many. Both therefore ought to have power, that each may defend itself against the other." The founders had such thoughts in mind when they designed the Senate, a small long-serving body, that would attract the rich, and the House, a large drive-through one, for the less rich.

This was an abstract problem of political theory. As practical economists, the founders often denied that there were truly poor people in America at all. Thomas Jefferson assured one correspondent that "we have no paupers." The founders believed this, in part, because they seldom noticed their own slaves when they were considering such matters (a Polish visitor to Mount Vernon commented that the slave quarters, though better than others he had seen in Virginia, were "more miserable" than the worst cottages of Polish peasants).

But when the founders went to Europe, they were genuinely shocked by the degradation they saw there. Jefferson lived in France in the late 1780s, a time of bad weather and bad harvests. One day he had a conversation with a woman farmworker in the town of Fontainebleau, site of the king's hunting lodge. She told him of her hard life, and when he gave her a small coin that was three times her daily wage, she burst into tears of gratitude.

Disturbed, Jefferson sent his friend and sounding board James Madison some thoughts on how to lessen such crushing disparities of wealth. He suggested breaking up huge estates by abolishing primogeniture—laws restricting inheritance to eldest sons—and levying progressive taxes. Then his mind took flight. "The earth is given as a common stock for man to labor and live on." Society legalizes property as an incentive to work. But "we must take care that other employment be provided to those" who have no property at all. "If we do not, the fundamental right to labor the earth returns to the unemployed." Jefferson's speculations had no practical consequences. Primogeniture had already been abolished in Virginia (with Jefferson's help), and he never pushed progressive taxation or his idea of the earth as a common stock. He believed that there was more equality of both opportunity and result in America than in Europe, and he hoped the cheap land of the frontier would keep it so.

The founder who spoke most directly to the poor was Benjamin Franklin. The advice he gave them was the same advice he gave everybody—work hard. For twenty-five years, Franklin printed a series of almanacs under the name Richard Saunders (Poor Richard). In 1757, he gathered together the maxims he had scattered throughout them. This essay, called "The Way to Wealth," endlessly reprinted and translated into numerous languages, was the most popular thing Franklin published during his lifetime.

"The Way to Wealth" is a secular sermon, supposedly delivered by an old man, Father Abraham, to a crowd of shoppers awaiting the start of a sale. His speech is a medley of one-liners, the greatest hits of Industry, Frugality, and Attention to Business. "Early to bed, and early to rise, makes a man healthy, wealthy and wise." "The sleeping fox catches no poultry." "Diligence is the mother of good luck." "At the working man's house, Hunger looks in, but dares not enter." "The Indies have not made Spain rich, because her outgoes are greater than her incomes." "A small leak will sink a great ship." "Keep thy shop, and thy shop will keep thee." "If you would have a faithful servant, and one you like, serve yourself." Anyone who follows these precepts will rise in the world. "A ploughman on his legs is higher than a gentleman on his knees." Anyone who ignores them will sink. "Pride breakfasted with plenty, dined with poverty, and supped with infamy." When Father Abraham finished, Franklin wrote with a saving wink, the audience "approved the doctrine" and immediately forgot it, for the minute the sale opened, "they began to buy extravagantly." Many a capitalist, from Robert Morris on down, ignored the advice too.

Thus Franklin the moralist. At the same time, Franklin the institution builder helped found the Pennsylvania Hospital. In the eighteenth century prosperous people saw their doctors at home; hospitals were for the poor. THIS BUILDING, Franklin wrote on the cornerstone, BY THE BOUNTY OF THE GOVERNMENT, AND OF MANY PRIVATE PERSONS, WAS PIOUSLY FOUNDED, FOR THE RELIEF OF THE SICK AND MISERABLE. MAY THE GOD OF MERCIES BLESS THE UNDERTAKING!

When Thomas Paine looked, like Jefferson, at European poverty, he came up with even more radical notions. Paine, an English immigrant, wrote a plan of reform for his former country in 1792. Paine wanted annual payments to poor families with children, and to the elderly poor (old age for Paine began at fifty: "though the mental faculties of man are in full vigour, and his judgment better than at any preceeding date, the bodily powers for laborious life are on the decline"). He proposed to fund his social spending from disarmament, progressive taxes on land, and slashing the payrolls of the government and the royal family. "Is it then better that the lives of one hundred and forty thousand aged persons be rendered comfortable, or that a million [pounds] a year of public money be expended on any one individual, and him often of the most worthless or insignificant character?" Several of Paine's assumptions were unrealistic, to put it mildly: he suggested merging the navies of Britain, France, and Holland as a cost-cutting measure, at a time when the three countries were on the brink of a world war. He did not think his reforms were needed in America, because republican government was less extravagant. President Washington, Paine wrote, would not accept a salary of a million pounds a year. "His sense of honour is of another kind."

Self-help and charity were the welfare program of the founders.

Would the Founders Have Drilled in ANWR?

The founders looked at the natural world with a mixture of wonder, scientific curiosity, and profit maximizing. The continent beyond the Alleghenies seemed boundless, barely comprehensible. Only a few military men among them—George Washington, George Rogers Clark, Anthony Wayne—had seen any of it personally. James Thomas Flexner, a Washington biographer who was also an art historian, noted that Washington's taste as a collector of paintings ran to wilderness scenes, as if he wanted Hudson River School views before the Hudson River School existed. President Jefferson's Corps of Discovery, the Lewis and Clark expedition, mixed science and romance. Jefferson had long hoped to find evidence of huge North American beasts, to refute European scientists who asserted that all life forms shriveled in the

New World; he once thought he had some bones of a gigantic lion, though they turned out to be the remains of a prehistoric sloth.

In their daily lives, the founders and their fellow Americans approached the natural world in a utilitarian spirit. They cleared, farmed, and in many cases exhausted the soil of the East Coast as fast as they could. They mined iron wherever it was found; the Pine Barrens of New Jersey, now a wilderness halfway between Philadelphia and New York, was once thick with foundries. Alexander Hamilton expressed the utilitarian spirit with blunt gusto in his *Report on Manufactures*. Economies based on manufacturing, he wrote approvingly, exploit natural resources more efficiently. "The bowels as well as the surface of the earth are ransacked for articles which were before neglected. Animals, plants and minerals acquire an utility and value, which were before unexplored." One of Hamilton's legal clients, William Cooper, put his talk about plants into action. He developed Cooperstown in upstate New York, brought in forty thousand settlers, and told the world that maple sugar would replace cane sugar from the Caribbean. It didn't; Cooper's heirs went bankrupt.

The founders believed in property rights as a way of ordering society, and stimulating growth and good character. Even Paine at his most radical acknowledged that it would be "impolitic to set bounds to property acquired by industry." Confronted with environmental pressures that they had not imagined, they might well be inclined to let the market manage scarcity. But their faith in property was not unlimited, for they recognized the Roman principle that the safety of the people is the supreme law.

A few years after leaving the White House, Jefferson recalled an incident during the Battle of Germantown when Washington's troops came under fire from British soldiers holed up in a mansion belonging to a Philadelphia judge. Washington "did not hesitate to plant his cannon against it, though the property of a citizen. When he besieged Yorktown," Jefferson went on, "he leveled the suburbs, feeling that the laws of property must be postponed to the safety of the nation." These were wartime emergencies, but Jefferson generalized the principle. "A ship at sea in distress for provisions, meets another having abundance, yet refusing a supply; the law of self-preservation authorizes the distressed to take a supply by force. In all these cases, the unwritten laws of necessity, of self-preservation, and of public safety, control the written laws of *meum* and *tuum* [mine and thine]."

Jefferson was writing about one-shot violations of the law. But if his principle could cover both wartime and peacetime emergencies, it could also cover chronic crises. If the founders were convinced that economic necessity required drilling on public land, or that environmental necessity forbade private companies from drilling on their own land, they would not hesitate to legislate accordingly. Since several of them, including Jefferson, were scientifically inclined, they would need good proof.

Would the Founders Believe in Building Infrastructure?

The late eighteenth century was the dawn of the heyday of canal building. George Washington wanted to develop the Potomac as an artery into the interior of America, and talked about it constantly at Mount Vernon. "The General sent the bottle around pretty freely after dinner," wrote one guest, "and gave success to the navigation of the Potomac for his toast." "The persuasive tongue of this great man," wrote another guest, ". . . completely infected me with the canal mania." In 1795 Gouverneur Morris saw the Forth and Clyde Canal in Scotland, a newly built waterway that connected the country's east and west coasts. "When I see this," he wrote in his diary, "my mind opens to a view of wealth for the interior of America." Twenty years later, he urged New York State to begin the Erie Canal.

What about canals that crossed state lines? Long after Hamilton and Madison became enemies, they agreed that the federal government should support such projects. Canals, wrote Hamilton in 1799, would "assist commerce and agriculture by rendering the transportation of commodities more cheap and expeditious," and "secure" national unity "by facilitating the communication between distant portions of the Union." "No objects within the circle of political economy so richly repay the expense bestowed on them," President Madison told Congress in 1815. "None . . . do more honor to the government whose wise and enlarged patriotism duly appreciates them." Hamilton and Madison agreed on another point: the Constitution would have to be amended to allow the federal government to build canals. The loose constructionist and the strict constructionist both thought that federally funded canals could not be construed from the Constitution as it stood. It was left to later generations to abandon their scruples.

Would the Founders Favor the Fed?

Everyone likes the Federal Reserve System these days, partly because it seems to work so well. (Not one person in a thousand ever thinks of it, a rough definition of working well.) But suspicion of public banks could revive at any time, for the same reasons that many of the founders were suspicious of them—most people (the founders included) do not understand banks or banking, and some bankers are in fact crooks.

Modern public banking was still relatively new in the founders' lifetimes. At the beginning of the eighteenth century, France had a disastrous experiment with it. John Law, a gambler if not an actual crook, established a national bank to restore France's finances after the wars of Louis XIV. But Law extended credit to an absurd extent, and crashed. The S&L bubble of the 1980s was a similar debacle.

Many founders, who were lawyers or planters by trade, looked on bankers as mysterious sharpies. Foreign bankers provoked John Adams into the only anti-Semitic utterance of his life: "Jews and Judaizing Christians," he wrote when he was a diplomat in England, were "scheeming to buy up all our continental notes at two or three shillings in a pound." (To his credit, Adams never pursued that particular train of thought, which snowballed through history without his assistance.) As an old man, Thomas Jefferson recalled proudly how he had been hated by American bankers: "I was derided as a maniac by the tribe of bank-mongers, who were seeking to filch from the public their swindling, and barren gains."

One of few founders who understood public banks was Alexander Hamilton, who asked Congress to charter a Bank of the United States in 1791. Hamilton knew why banks made people paranoid. "The necessary secrecy of their transactions gives unlimited scope to imagination to infer that something is, or may be wrong." He lifted the veil to explain how banks could issue loans in excess of their deposits. "It is a well established fact, that banks in good credit can circulate a far greater sum than the actual quantum of their capital in Gold & Silver." A bank could get away with this because customers would not withdraw their deposits all at once, so long as the bank was known to be trustworthy. A public bank earned trust when it was run as a private-sector institution, not an ATM of the government. "The keen, steady, and, as it were, magnetic sense" of the directors' self-interest is "the only security, that can always be relied upon, for a careful and prudent administration." If the government extended too much credit, then self-interest flowed in the direction of quick killings, and a train wreck like Law's is the result.

The Bank of the United States was chartered for twenty years. Jefferson complained about it when he became president: the bank, he wrote his treasury secretary, Albert Gallatin, was "deadly hostil[e]" to the principles of the Constitution. But Gallatin found the bank useful, and when its charter came up for renewal in 1811, he and President Madison wanted to extend its life. The House approved, the Senate tied, and Vice President George Clinton, a more consistent Jeffersonian than Jefferson's heirs, broke the tie in the negative.

A year later, the United States went to war against Great Britain, with essentially no money, and nowhere to borrow it. Governments don't need loans if they vow never to spend or fight.

What Would the Founders Do about Social Security?

Some of the founders lived to great ages. John Adams (1735–1826) was the longest-lived ex-president, until Ronald Reagan (1911–2004) edged him out. They knew the consolations of age—grandchildren, old friends, setting the world to rights—but they also knew the aches, pains, and tedium. In "the hoary winter of age," wrote Thomas Jefferson, when he was eighty-one, "we can think of nothing but how to keep ourselves warm, and how to get rid of our heavy hours until the friendly hand of death shall rid us of all at once."

The founders expected the old to be taken care of by their families. The expectation was so strong that Jefferson even argued that old people without families were "too few to merit notice as a separate section of society." Failing family care, the indigent old had to rely on the local charities, such as hospitals, established for the poor.

Two special classes of older people were otherwise provided for. Congress gave officers who served in the Revolutionary War pensions, though George Washington disliked the word: *pension* in the eighteenth century suggested a pay-off to a do-nothing hanger-on, whereas Washington believed the pension for officers "was the price of their blood and your independency, it is therefore more than a common debt, it is a debt of honour." Privates and noncoms who had been crippled also received pensions. "Nothing could be a more melancholy and distressing sight," Washington wrote, "than to behold those who have shed their blood or lost their limbs in the service of their Country . . . compelled to beg their daily bread from door to door!"

The other class of persons who were cared for in old age was slaves. Masters needed to think of themselves as biblical patriarchs, to avoid thinking of themselves as buyers and sellers of men. "Providence," wrote John Jay to his son, "has placed these persons in stations below us. They are servants but they are men; and kindness to inferiors . . . indicates magnanimity [rather] than meanness." Caring for slaves who could no longer work was a partial compensation for their masters' profit from a lifetime of free labor.

In his Last Will and Testament, written in 1799, Washington went further. After freeing all his slaves, he acknowledged that "among those who will receive freedom . . . there may be some, who from old age or bodily infirmities . . . will be unable to support themselves." He directed that these former slaves "be comfortably cloathed and fed by my heirs while they live," and he required his executors to establish "a regular and permanent fund . . . for their Support," since he did not trust "the uncertain provision to be made by individuals." The Washington estate paid out pensions until 1833. Slaves are not trained to be freemen; Washington accepted the necessity of providing for those who had been marked by their upbringing.

The founders provided yet another way of receiving payments from the federal government, for young and old alike, foreigners as well as Americans: buying a share of the national debt. Alexander Hamilton's *Report on Public Credit* included a discussion of the annuities that he proposed to offer, and their different rates of return. Like a good salesman, he created the impression that the train was leaving the station. "The advantages" of investing in America "have already engaged the attention of the European moneylenders. . . . [A]s they become better understood, they will have the greater influence."

Social Security follows none of these models (family provision, charity, reward for service, investment). It is a payback on a mandatory tax, funded by younger taxpayers. If the founders could have accepted such a program, how would they keep it going as the pool of retirees grew, and the pool of younger taxpayers grew more slowly? What would they think about the ensuing debt?

Most of the founders had a strange relation to debt, both personal and public. They feared it, often extravagantly: Washington classed defaulters with pickpockets and the emperor Nero. But as often happens, those who most feared something nevertheless fell into its clutches, as if under hypnosis. Robert Morris, the titan of commerce, went bankrupt, but so did Thomas Jefferson, the apostle of rural life. Morris was part of the new economic world, Jefferson firmly rooted in the old one, yet both suffered the same fate (Morris's solution to bad investments was to make new ones, many of which also turned out to be bad; Jefferson noted every penny of income and outflow, but never learned to balance his books).

One of the only founders with a sophisticated understanding of modern debt financing was Hamilton. "The proper funding" of debt, he wrote, "render[s] it a national blessing," by fortifying the government's credit. Yet he warned that "the creation of debt should always be accompanied with the means of extinguishment." Otherwise, the government would be tempted to "prodigality" and "dangerous abuse." Debt financing could multiply an economy's resources, but you always had to show an ability to pay. Hamilton knew that a government never acts in a vacuum. The same investors who hold its IOUs watch its behavior; if it misbehaves, its credit rating sinks. "When the credit of a country is in any degree questionable, it never fails to give an extravagant premium . . . upon all the loans it has occasion to make."

If the rules of a government program were leading it toward disaster, Hamilton would change the rules.

Would the Founders Back State-Sponsored Gambling?

In February 1826, the last year of his life, Thomas Jefferson asked the Virginia legislature to authorize a lottery. In his petition, he analyzed the morality of games of chance. His first point was startling. "If we consider games of chance immoral, then every pursuit of human industry is immoral; for there is not a single one that is not subject to chance." Captains risk their ships, and merchants risk their cargoes; farmers bet on the weather, builders bet on the real estate market, hunters bet on the prevalence of game. "These, then, are games of chance. Yet so far from being immoral, they are indispensable to the existence of man." In one swoop, he overturned all Benjamin Franklin's almanac maxims about hard work.

His second thought was more cautious. Trade, farming, and the rest produce real goods when the bet pays off. But games of chance that were pure diversions—Jefferson specified cards, dice, and billiards—"are entirely unproductive." They were also "so seducing . . . to men of a certain constitution of mind, that they cannot resist the temptation" of betting on them. In such cases, "as in those of insanity, idiocy, infancy, etc., it is the duty of society to take" gambling addicts "under its protection; even against their own acts, and to restrain their right of choice of these pursuits, by suppressing them entirely." Jefferson the libertarian saw chance everywhere; Jefferson the republican saw the damage that the pursuit of it sometimes did. The two Jeffersons dueled till the end.

Jefferson concluded that lotteries belonged to a third class of games of chance—those that were harmful if they became habitual, but "useful on certain occasions." The Virginia legislature therefore had the right to permit lotteries on a case-by-case basis, and had done so, Jefferson pointed out, for seventy worthy causes from 1782 to 1820, from helping the College of William and Mary to improving the road to Snigger's Gap.

The purpose of Jefferson's petition was poignant: he was one hundred thousand dollars in debt (almost two million dollars today). He wanted the legislature to permit him to hold a lottery to liquidate part of his estate, in order to save the rest. He was asking for special treatment, and he knew it; one cause of his troubles was the depressed condition of agriculture in Virginia, but every farmer suffered from that. (Another cause of his troubles—his inability to economize—was not something he cared to face, hence, perhaps, his insistence that all economic pursuits are games of chance.) The legislature balked, then relented. Jefferson died in July 1826, hopeful that his heirs would keep something, but the lottery was not a success. His estate was auctioned off six months later.

CHAPTER 6

War and Peace

PEOPLE don't go to war as often as they go to work, but war
intrudes on all but the shortest lives. The founders lived in a
world of war. In 1740, George Washington, age eight, saw his first
uniform when his elder brother went off to fight in the War of
Jenkins' Ear. In 1836, Aaron Burr, age eighty, claimed that the
schemes that got him tried for treason had finally been fulfilled
by the Texas War of Independence.

The Revolutionary War was the longest war America fought
until Vietnam—longer than the Civil War and our participation
in World War II put together—and it shaped a generation of
leaders. When Washington had to deal with the Whiskey Rebellion, he consulted with his secretaries of war, treasury, and state;
his attorney general; and the governors of Pennsylvania and Virginia. All of them had been officers in the Revolution. Winning,

waging, and avoiding wars were major concerns of the founders' statecraft, their politicking, and, in many cases, their careers.

What Would the Founders Do about Terrorism?

Eighteenth-century warfare was supposed to be a civilized affair, with elaborate rules for how prisoners should be treated, exchanged, or paroled. When the British lost the Battle of Saratoga in 1778, the American commander, General Horatio Gates, signed a convention allowing General John Burgoyne and his men to go home, so long as they promised not to return to fight again in America. The terms caused some grumbling, since the homecoming enemy would free up other troops to replace them. But before Burgoyne could sail away, he unwisely complained of the temporary accommodations the Americans gave him, which allowed them to claim that he had rejected the convention and to hold his men prisoner.

Such were the rules, and often the practice. But war shaded into terror, especially when it was fought in remote or chaotic areas. Frontier warfare, involving Indian allies and enemies, was brutal on both sides. Joseph Brant, a.k.a. Thayendenegea, was a Mohawk chief who led murderous raids on patriot farmers in New York and Pennsylvania, killing women and children as well as soldiers. Brant was no savage—he was a devout Episcopalian who helped translate the Gospel of Mark into Mohawk—he simply behaved savagely in wartime. George Washington responded by sending General John Sullivan to destroy the Indians' towns, crops, and "everything that was to be found." Sullivan, who had the help of friendly Oneidas, laid forty villages to waste; Brant's raids only redoubled.

In the South, guerrilla warfare raged between patriots and loyalists. General Nathanael Greene, sent to retrieve the military situation in the Carolinas in 1781, wrote in shock to his wife, Caty, about what he found there. "The sufferings and distress of the inhabitants beggars [*sic*] all description. . . . [T]hey persecute each other with little less than savage fury." Recently, the historian David Hackett Fischer has popularized an ethnic theory of southern exceptionalism to explain such conduct: southerners fight ferociously because they always have, back to their pre-immigration days in Ulster and the Scotch-English border. There is something to this, but the American Revolution became vicious wherever neither side clearly controlled territory and fighting fell by default to bands of irregulars. Westchester County, north of British-occupied New York, was another such no-man's land; there the marauders were called cowboys.

Early in the war, General Charles Lee, a radical, eccentric English officer who had settled in Virginia and taken up the American cause, envisioned a guerrilla struggle, involving punitive measures against American loyalists. Native-born officers like Washington and Greene preferred to rely on a professional army, responsible to the politicians in Congress. No doubt they were motivated, in part, by pride: they wanted to show the enemy, their former rulers, that they were not rubes leading some ragtag uprising. But they also dreaded the civil commotion that Lee evidently welcomed.

Washington and Greene were right. John Adams guessed that a third of the American people supported the Revolution, a third opposed it, and a third were indifferent. The key factor in shifting those numbers as the war progressed was the brutal conduct of pro-British irregulars. Since the British army controlled less territory, they were more reliant on such help. The Americans didn't always do right, but they did right more often than their enemies, and it did them a lot of good.

What Would the Founders Do about Rogue States?

The founders knew four rogue states: the Muslim principalities of North Africa, or the Barbary Coast—Morocco, Algiers, Tunis, and Tripoli (Libya). These countries ran a naval protection racket in the Mediterranean, demanding tribute from civilized nations; if any country did not pay up front, they captured its ships and enslaved the crews, holding them for ransom. The infant United States paid tribute, along with all the more powerful European powers. No one doubted that Admiral Nelson or his French counterparts could smash the Barbary navies in one cruise. But Nelson and the French were otherwise engaged, fighting each other. Even in peacetime, the costs of punishment might outweigh the benefits. In 1801 Yussuf Karamanli, the bashaw of Tripoli—a man of "very splendid and tawdry appearance"— became the first foreign ruler to declare war on the United States, hoping to extort higher payments.

Thomas Jefferson, newly inaugurated as president, wanted to shrink the navy, which he considered extravagant. But he also resented the idea of paying either tribute or ransom. He sent almost all the small navy he had to the Mediterranean, to deal with Karamanli.

There were setbacks—the frigate *Philadelphia* ran aground on a reef in Tripoli harbor and had to be burned; the crew was enslaved. There were also successes: the Americans took the bashaw's second-largest town, Derne (Darnah), with a combined sea-land assault. The land assault was particularly heroic: a five hundred–mile march through the desert from Egypt by a party of marines, mercenaries, and Muslim allies, led by an impetuous diplomat, William Eaton. (Eaton's exploit is remembered in the Marine Corps hymn: "to the shores of Tripoli.") Jefferson kept several options open. He might depose Karamanli and replace him with his older brother, or he might intimidate him into striking a better deal. Once Eaton was in Derne and the U.S. Navy was before Tripoli, the bashaw saw reason, and returned all his American slaves for sixty thousand dollars, not the cool million he had originally demanded.

Jefferson congratulated himself on his victory, but it was only temporary. America was soon embroiled with Britain, the greatest maritime power on earth, and the Barbary states resumed the pirate business. In 1815 a new American squadron sailed to the Mediterranean, compelling Algiers, Tunis, and Tripoli to forswear piracy and to pay damages for past offenses. President Madison hailed "this demonstration of American skill and prowess." America was off the hook, but piracy did not finally end until France and the Ottoman Empire occupied the entire Barbary Coast.

Then as now, the three ways of dealing with rogue states were negotiation, force, and overwhelming force.

What Would the Founders Do about WMD?

The founders had no notion of atomic or chemical weapons, but they knew one biological weapon: deliberate infection by smallpox.

The stratagem was considered by the British during Pontiac's rebellion in 1763, an aftershock of the French and Indian War. "Could it not be contrived," wrote Sir Jeffrey Amherst, the British commander, "to send the small pox among those disaffected tribes of Indians?" At the same time, an English trader wrote that two Indian chiefs visiting Fort Pitt (now Pittsburgh) had been given "two blankets and an handkerchief out of the small pox hospital. I hope it will have the desired effect." There was a smallpox outbreak among the Indians of the Ohio Valley shortly thereafter.

Did the British consider germ warfare against Americans as well as Native Americans? George Washington suspected the British might have done so while he besieged them in Boston in 1775. "I could not suppose them capable of" it, he wrote John Hancock, "[but] I now must give some credit to it as [smallpox] has made its appearance on several of those who last came out of Boston." At war's end, in 1781, General Alexander Leslie suggested to Lord Cornwallis that slaves fleeing from rebel plantations who had smallpox be sent back, in order to infect their masters. Years later, an American soldier who had fought at Yorktown remembered seeing "in the woods herds of Negroes" suffering from smallpox, "turned adrift . . . dead and dying, with pieces of ears of Indian corn in the hands and mouths."

Did talk lead to action? Did action have consequences? Smallpox raged throughout North America during the late eighteenth century; it didn't need to be spread by blankets from Fort Pitt. Leslie's plan twenty years later may never have borne fruit, any more than Herman Kahn's nuclear war–gaming did. But the spirit was willing to use disease to weaken the enemy's flesh. We also do not necessarily know everything the British might have done in Pontiac's Rebellion or the American Revolution, since seventeenth- and eighteenth-century theorists of the laws of war had laid down the principle that women and children were not legitimate targets. Practitioners of germ warfare thus had reason to conceal what they were doing.

Washington had caught smallpox when he was nineteen years old, giving him a lifetime immunity. During the Valley Forge winter, he inoculated the American army by infecting his soldiers with smallpox under controlled conditions. (The inoculation had to be administered secretly, lest the British attack while the Americans were understrength.) Washington saved his troops from nature and from the enemy. As Benjamin Franklin said in another context, "An ounce of prevention is worth a pound of cure."

Would the Founders Consider Conscription?

All soldiers in the regular army during the founding period were volunteers, fighting for some combination of patriotism, pay, and excitement. One veteran of the Revolutionary War described how he signed up, age fifteen, two days after the Declaration of Independence:

> I found a number of young men of my acquaintance [at the recruiting station]. The old bantering began—come, if you will enlist I will, says one; you have long been talking about it, says another—come, now is the time. . . . So seating myself at the table, enlisting orders were immediately presented to me; I took up the pen, loaded it with the fatal charge, made several mimic imitations of writing my name, but took especial care not to touch the paper with the pen until an unlucky wight [fellow] who was leaning over my shoulder gave my hand a stroke, which caused the pen to make a woeful scratch on the paper. "O, he has enlisted," said he. "He has made his mark; he is fast enough now." Well, thought I, I may as well go through with the business now as not. So I wrote my name fairly.

With one brief break, he stayed in the army for the next seven years. So it goes—frivolously, and seriously—today.

There was one form of conscription in the founding period. Every county was supposed to periodically drill its able-bodied men, whom the state could summon in emergencies to fight wars, or suppress domestic unrest. These forces were called the militia. A militia could be useful in emergencies, if it was well led. But holiday drilling was not the same as regular discipline, and the militia's effectiveness suffered accordingly.

Founders who were in positions of military authority seriously considered drafting men into the regular army, both in the American Revolution and in the War of 1812. In December 1775, George Washington, besieging the British in Boston, asked Congress and the New England states to order "every town to provide a certain quota of men for the campaign." In October 1814, Secretary of War James Monroe, who had vainly tried to prevent the British from burning Washington, D.C., two months earlier, asked Congress to triple the army by a draft. "Congress ha[s] a right by the Constitution to raise regular armies, and no restraint is imposed on the exercise of it. . . . It would be absurd to suppose that Congress could not carry this power into effect [except by relying on] the voluntary service of individuals."

In both cases, Congress balked. Opposition was especially vehement during the unpopular War of 1812. One senator called Monroe's plan "odious," while Thomas Jefferson, observing the debate from Monticello, wrote that "we might as well rely on calling down an army of angels from heaven." Jefferson was motivated by principled dislike of regular armies. Monroe's congressional critics, mostly from New England, were motivated by a treasonous desire to secede from the Union; they fulminated against conscription as a wedge issue to make secession attractive.

Founders who had fighting responsibility thought conscription should be an option, but it would not become a feature of American life until long after they were gone.

Would the Founders Fight Preemptive Wars?

When President Jefferson bought the Louisiana Territory from France in 1803 for fifteen million dollars, his Federalist opponents weren't pleased. What was good for him, they reasoned, was bad for the country. Alexander Hamilton made a partial exception, writing in the *New-York Evening Post* that the purchase was "an important acquisition," even though it would "give éclat" (good buzz) to the Jefferson administration. Hamilton's only quibble was that Jefferson should have taken Louisiana outright. France, which had come under the control of Napoleon Bonaparte, had been preventing Americans from shipping goods down the Mississippi River. Since the American right to use the Mississippi was guaranteed by treaty, Hamilton thought interference was a "justifiable cause of war." We should have seized New Orleans "at once"; if we then decided to buy it, we could have set the price.

If preemptive war means attacking another country before it attacks us, then Hamilton was in favor of it. But if preemptive war means attacking another country without good reason, then he moves out of the pro column.

Would the Founders Accuse Each Other of Being Chicken Hawks?

After the Revolution, Henry Knox had an idea: there should be an association of veteran officers to keep the memory of their service green. The organization would have fourteen chapters—one for each state, and one for France. Naturally, George Washington, the former commander in chief, would preside.

The name that was chosen—the Society of the Cincinnati—emphasized its status as a group of nonprofessional soldiers. Cincinnatus was a half-mythical figure of early Roman history, a farmer who had left his plow to defend the state against invaders, then returned to it when the war ended. Corrupt countries might have permanent military establishments, but the Society of the Cincinnati would honor our citizen officers.

The plan caused intense alarm. American life was so local and scattered that there were no other private organizations that spanned the nation (even churches were regionally concentrated). Was the Society of the Cincinnati a peacetime veterans' plot to run the country? Washington was so concerned by the talk that he begged off attending the society's meeting in Philadelphia in the summer of 1787. He was then briefly perplexed when the Constitutional Convention, which required his presence, was scheduled for Philadelphia at the same time. He stiffed the Cincinnati and went to the convention. There, the Cincinnati were a topic of discussion. Elbridge Gerry warned that a "set of men, dispersed through the union and acting in concert," would control presidential elections. "Such a society of men existed in the order of the Cincinnati. . . . His respect for the characters composing this society could not blind him to the danger and impropriety of throwing such a power into their hands."

Gerry had reason for his fears. The man on horseback was the traditional enemy of republics. Julius Caesar tried to overthrow the Roman Republic. Cromwell supplanted Parliament after the English Civil War. In the founders' own lifetime,

Napoleon would replace the French Republic (Thomas Jefferson called his rule a "maniac tyranny"). Good republicans were shocked by the notion that public life should be conducted by current or former soldiers. As first president general of the Society of the Cincinnati, Washington modified its bylaws to make it seem less threatening.

Yet republicans are also men, and war has a powerful hold on men's minds. "Oh, that I was a soldier!" John Adams wrote Abigail in 1775. "I will be. I am reading military books. Everyone must and will, and shall be a soldier." Adams had never been a soldier, even though he had lived through the French and Indian War, and he would never become one. His presidency threw his life history in his face. In 1797 he sent a three-man commission to try to repair our relations with France, which had been seizing American ships it suspected of carrying contraband to its enemy, Britain. After the commissioners arrived in Paris, the French negotiators demanded bribes ("You must pay money—you must pay a great deal of money") before the discussions could begin. When America learned of the norms of French diplomacy, the country blazed in indignation. War seemed inevitable, and we actually began engaging the French navy. "The finger of destiny," Adams declared, "writes on the wall the word: war!"

In time, however, Adams came to believe that the French were willing to talk in earnest (they had suffered various setbacks and wanted to clear one problem from the board). Adams, however, feared being labeled not a chicken hawk, but a chicken dove. How could a lifelong civilian back out of a war without his courage being questioned? John Ferling argues that Adams's psychic bind was eased when Washington, who had come out of retirement to command the American army in case of invasion, passed on to Adams another French peace feeler that had found its way to Mount Vernon. If Washington, first in war, was a hawk dove, then Adams could pursue peace with a clean conscience.

The European war went on, as did assaults on our shipping. In 1812 President Madison, another lifelong civilian, asked Congress to declare war on Britain. This time, there was no Washington to come out of retirement to lead our army. America touched bottom in 1814 when a British expeditionary force sailed up Chesapeake Bay and moved on Washington, D.C. A badly led American army met the invaders at Bladensburg, Maryland, a mile outside the district's limits. President Madison, sixty-three years old, borrowed a pistol and rode out to the field. It was a brave gesture from a small, hypochondriac intellectual. Secretary of War James Monroe, who had been a colonel in the Revolution, advised the president to leave before the shooting started, so as not to be a distraction. The battle, like so many others before it, was a disaster. Madison's wife, Dolley, left the White House a step ahead of the victorious British, taking a portrait of Washington lest the enemy burn it; they did burn the White House.

The founders admired men on horseback and rode on horseback themselves when they had to, even as they maintained a republican suspicion of the military. The most important mark of honor to their minds was not battlefield experience, but republican ideals.

Did the Founders Believe in Special Relationships with Foreign Countries?

America's relations with Britain have gone through three phases: parent-child, enemies, intimates. The period of fraternal cooperation, which began in the mid-1890s, is often called the "special relationship." (Winston Churchill coined the phrase in his 1946 speech at Westminster College in Fulton, Missouri, the same in which he also spoke of the "iron curtain.") The United States is sometimes said to have special relationships—friendly or hostile—with other countries (Israel, France, Canada, Mexico).

Thomas Jefferson's first inaugural address (1801) offered "peace, commerce and honest friendship with all nations—entangling alliances with none." George Washington's Farewell Address (1796) made a more sweeping statement of national detachment: "'Tis our true policy to steer clear of permanent alliances with any portion of the foreign world." Jefferson forswore entangling alliances; Washington thought any permanent alliance would entangle.

Washington warned against permanent alliances for two reasons. He didn't expect to gain any special benefits from allies, beyond what was in their interests at any particular time: "'Tis folly in one Nation to look for disinterested favors from another. . . . There can be no greater error than to expect, or calculate upon real favours from nation to nation." He also feared the effects of permanent alliances, or enmities, on American policy makers and citizens. "Inveterate antipathies against particular nations and passionate attachments for others should be excluded." The former breeds unnecessary ill-will, and the latter breeds favoritism. Both lead to a loss of judgment, and of self-control. "The nation, which indulges towards another an habitual hatred, or an habitual fondness, is in some degree a slave"—a charged word for a slave owner to use. "It is a slave to its animosity or to its affection, either of which is sufficient to lead it astray from its duty and its interest."

Washington was influenced by the events of his administration. Months after his first inauguration in 1789, the Bastille fell.

In a short time, France, which had helped us win our independence, had become a crusading revolutionary state. Should the treaty we had signed during the Revolutionary War with Louis XVI be honored with the men who deposed, then killed, him? Thomas Jefferson, James Madison, and their followers approved of the French Revolution, and thought a failure to be friendly with France would be truckling to our former enemy, Britain. Washington wanted to steer a neutral course and, with considerable risk to his own popularity, managed to do it. (France's bumptious behavior helped him. The French ambassador, "Citizen" Edmond-Charles Genet, tried to appeal to the American people over Washington's head, which even Jefferson thought was a terrible idea.)

But Washington was also influenced by the course of his life. The first enemies he killed in battle were Frenchmen, as a twenty-two-year-old colonel in the French and Indian War. Twenty years later, he was fighting the British with French help; Lafayette became his spiritual son. On his watch as president, France had become menacing again. He had seen the wheel turn twice. No doubt it would keep spinning.

Washington's ghost writer on the Farewell Address was Alexander Hamilton, whose enemies accused him, with reason, of being pro-British. In 1789, at the beginning of his tenure as treasury secretary, Hamilton had a private chat with George Beckwith, a British operative, in which he said, "I have always preferred a connexion with you, to that of any other country. *We think in English.*" Hamilton was angling for better commercial relations—and the customs revenues that would flow from them—when he said this. But whenever the British were overbearing during the Washington administration—the great powers seemed almost to be hazing the young one—Hamilton advised the president to push back. Like Washington, he was un-sentimental about countries. "The predominant motive of good offices [deeds] from one nation to another is the interest or ad-vantage of the nation which performs them."

Jefferson, the unnamed target of Washington's Farewell Ad-dress, had placed extravagant hopes on the French Revolution. "The liberty of the whole earth was depending on the issue of the contest," he wrote in 1793, at the depths of the Reign of Terror. "Rather than it should have failed, I would have seen half the earth desolated." But even Jefferson's enthusiasm had limits, and he reached them with Napoleon. When the young general took power in a coup late in 1799, Jefferson called it "painfully interest-ing." Napoleon was a military swaggerer, exactly the kind of per-son Jefferson most disliked. By the time of his inauguration, in March 1801, he was criticizing "entangling alliances." A year later, when he feared that Napoleon might not sell him the Louisiana Territory, he told his negotiator, Robert Livingston, that in that case "we must marry ourselves to the British fleet" in order to take it. Jefferson had learned Washington's lesson.

Would the Founders Use Covert Ops?

William Eaton, the man who invaded the pirate state of Tripoli in order to drive one brother from the throne and put another in his place (see "What Would the Founders Do about Rogue States?" above), was a covert operative. Nominally, he was the American consul in Tunis, but he had been assigned his military mission by Thomas Jefferson and James Madison, president and secretary of state. "To intermeddle in the domestic contests of other countries," Madison observed, "does not accord with the general sentiments or views of the United States." Yet "it cannot be unfair, in the prosecution of a just war . . . to turn to [our] advantage the enmity . . . of others against a common foe." Ultimately, Jefferson and Madison chose to go the diplomatic route, forcing Eaton to leave Tripoli's territory, and leaving his candidate for the throne hanging.

George Washington as commander in chief was a great believer in spies. On the eve of the Battle of Trenton, he wrote Robert Morris, member of Congress and one of the richest men in North America, "We have the greatest occasion [need] at present for hard money, to pay a certain set of people who are particular use to us. . . . Silver would be most convenient." There is a legend that Washington used a double agent, a gigantic weaver named John Honeyman, to feed misinformation to the Hessian garrison in Trenton. Skeptics point out that the story rests on family tradition only, and lacks independent documentary proof. Believers ask, since when do commanders in chief keep records of their covert ops?

The founders discouraged freelancers—covert operatives working on their own—even if the freelancers were founders themselves. In 1797, William Blount, signer of the Constitution and senator from Tennessee, was expelled from the Senate for cooking up a plan to liberate Spanish possessions in Louisiana and Florida with Indian and British help (as though Bill Frist were stirring up revolt in Cancun). In 1807, former vice president Aaron Burr was tried for treason, on the grounds that he had sailed down the Ohio and Mississippi Rivers with one hundred armed men, intending to seize power in New Orleans. (Burr had told at least some of his friends that he intended to attack the Spaniards in Texas instead.) He was acquitted, but his reputation was ruined.

Founding covert ops needed the approval of their higher-ups, even if the higher-ups intended to leave them in the lurch.

Did the Founders See America as an Example to the World?

If the advice of George Washington's Farewell Address (see "Did the Founders Believe in Special Relationships with Foreign Countries?" above) was correct, it had consequences. The United States would look out for its own interests, and every other country would do likewise. There would be no point in being an example for the world, since the world would have other things on its mind.

Yet, at the same time, the founders were tugged by the belief that they were actors on a larger stage—that their audience was the human race, and their time frame was all of time. In a forum like the Constitutional Convention, eternity could poke through the wrangles. If the delegates failed, Alexander Hamilton said at one point, the cause of republican government would be "disgraced and lost to mankind forever." "We shall disappoint not only America," Elbridge Gerry agreed, "but the whole world." Strange fears, strange hopes for a little country on the edge of nowhere. When America loses them, it will be far smaller.

Did the Founders Encourage Freedom Fighters in Other Countries?

The United States was always expecting Canada to join the fold. The Articles of Confederation provided (in Article 11) that Canada could enjoy "all the advantages of this union" whenever it liked; Canada never took up the offer. Early in the War of 1812,

Thomas Jefferson thought that the conquest of Canada, as far as Quebec, would be "a mere matter of marching"; we would snap up Halifax in Nova Scotia in 1813. In fact, the war on the American-Canadian frontier was a long, furious draw. There was little profit in looking for Canadian sympathizers.

If the founders did not encourage freedom fighters abroad, they benefited from foreigners who came here to fight alongside them. Most of these were professional soldiers from France and Spain, America's two major allies during the Revolution; however intrigued or sympathetic these men were, they would have gone anywhere they were sent. A few, though, stand out for their identification with the American cause.

Two, remarkably, were career soldiers. Baron von Steuben was a Prussian-born professional who instilled professionalism in the American army's organization and drill. Steuben's brilliance, however, was to intuit the American character, and to adapt his methods to it. Americans, he wrote, were not like "Prussians, Austrians or French. You say to [a European] soldier, 'Do this,' and he doeth it, but here I am obliged to say, 'This is the reason why you ought to do that' and then he does it." He simplified the European drill, and told his officers to show a personal interest in their men. Steuben never lost his accent, but he acquired an American mind-set, at least for the purposes of teaching his trade.

Baron Johann de Kalb, on the surface, was another lifer. Son of Bavarian peasants, he spent his career in the French army. In 1768 he was sent to the thirteen colonies as a spy to judge the prospects for revolt, and the potential opportunities for France. Kalb reported that the colonists were unhappy with British rule, but not ready for independence yet. When the revolution finally broke out, Kalb returned to fight. At the disastrous Battle of

Camden (1780) he stayed on the field long after the American commander, General Horatio Gates, had fled, and was bayoneted eleven times. The secret agent had embraced the cause.

Two Polish volunteers came in the midst of their own country's trials. Thaddeus Kosciusko was a military engineer who helped Nathanael Greene retake the Carolinas by supplying him with boats, to cross and recross the states' many rivers. Back in Poland after the Revolution, he fought vainly against its dismemberment by Russia and its other neighbors. Thomas Jefferson praised his "disinterested attachment to the freedom and happiness of man." Count Casimir Pulaski was a young cavalry officer who never lived to see his country disappear. "Here, by fighting for freedom, I wish to deserve it," he wrote Washington when he arrived in America in 1777. "Life or death for the welfare of the state is my motto." He was touchy and quarrelsome, but all was forgotten two years later when he died leading an infantry charge at the Battle of Savannah.

The model freedom fighter was the Marquis de Lafayette. He left his regiment, age nineteen, to "offer my services to the most interesting of Republics, bringing . . . only my candor and good will." When he met Washington at Valley Forge, the commander in chief made some apology for the condition of his troops. "I am here, sir, to learn," Lafayette said, "not to teach." The two immediately bonded. When the French Revolution broke out, Lafayette hoped to become the French Washington. His heart was pure—over the years he opposed the despotism of the king, the revolutionaries, Napoleon, and the restoration—but his judgment was often defective. He was made to serve, not to lead. America got the best of him; his best was very good.

Not all the foreign freedom fighters were heroes. Charles Lee (see "What Would the Founders Do about Terrorism?"

above) schemed behind Washington's back, and bungled an attack at the Battle of Monmouth so badly that he had to be relieved on the field. The Venezuelan Francisco de Miranda fought in a 1781 Spanish operation to drive the British out of Florida. He made a number of American friends, including Alexander Hamilton, and in later life he talked of liberating South America with their help, though he seemed equally intent on aggrandizing himself. Since fellow revolutionaries betrayed him to the Spanish, we will never know what sort of leader he would have made. Two future leaders of the Haitian revolution, André Rigaud and Henri Christophe, served as youths in a French West Indian unit at the Battle of Savannah, the same in which Pulaski died. Haiti's colonial experience, and its revolution, were far grimmer than ours. No one would envy Rigaud's and Christophe's opportunities; no one would admire their careers. Rigaud defended mulatto interests, and switched sides between the Haitians and the French. Christophe made himself King Henri I of northern Haiti, and committed suicide during a revolt.

People everywhere aspire to freedom, but not everyone is lucky enough to win it.

Would the Founders Support Spreading Democracy around the World?

In his second inaugural address, President George W. Bush declared it to be the United States' policy to "support the growth of democratic movements and institutions in every nation and culture." Before the founders addressed that point, they would first consider the wisdom of supporting the growth of democratic movements in the United States.

The Declaration states that just governments "deriv[e]" their powers "from the consent of the governed." (Unjust governments—for example, the British Empire under George III—derived their powers from monarchs, and the ministers and parliaments they had corrupted; the governed, whether in London or Boston, had no meaningful say in the matter.) But how is consent to be derived?

Neither the Articles of Confederation nor the Constitution set up direct democracies. (Under the articles, Congress was chosen by state legislatures; under the Constitution, the president, Congress, and federal judges are elected in various ways, or chosen by other elected officials.) James Madison justified these complications in *Federalist* no. 10, where he wrote a critical analysis of "pure democracy." In pure democracy nothing could restrain the "passion or interest" of majorities, which could be as hostile to liberty as George III. "Hence it is that [pure] democracies have ever been spectacles of turbulence and contention; have ever been incompatible with personal security or the rights of property; and have in general been as short in their lives as they have been violent in their deaths." His friend-turned-rival Alexander Hamilton was if anything even more skeptical of pure democracy. Hamilton did not, as many people believe, call the people "a great beast"—a bogus quote foisted on him by the historian Henry Adams, John's great-grandson, still carrying on the family's feuds eighty years after Hamilton was dead. But Hamilton did say, in the last letter he ever wrote, that "our real disease . . . is DEMOCRACY." Both men believed instead in filtering the popular will through layers of representation and different branches of government. "Is this . . . republican government?" Hamilton asked himself at the Constitutional Convention, then

WHAT WOULD THE FOUNDERS DO?

answered, "Yes, if all the magistrates are appointed, and vacancies filled, by the people, or a process of election originating with the people."

Thomas Jefferson was no pure democrat either; he served happily under the Constitution, and owed the margin of his first presidential victory in 1800 to the electoral votes of New York State, which had been chosen by the state legislature. But of all the founders he had the most confidence that popular opinion was essentially right. Though his political party was called the Republicans all his life, his optimism justified the name it ultimately took, and still carries: Democrats. Mankind, he wrote at the end of his life, divides naturally "into two parties: 1. Those who fear and distrust the people, and wish to draw all powers from them into the hands of the higher classes. 2. Those who identify themselves with the people, have confidence in them, cherish and consider them as the most honest and safe, although not the most wise depository of the public interests." His last-minute reservation about popular wisdom was no doubt prompted by the reflection that sometimes Party no. 1 had unaccountably come out on top. How had that happened? The people were fooled. By whom? By Jefferson's ancient enemies, closet Anglophiles and monarchists. Democrats are no more immune to conspiracy theories than anyone else.

Could democratic institutions work in countries that had never had them? In 1789 France began its revolution, grafting a popularly elected National Assembly onto an absolute monarchy. Hamilton observed it uneasily from New York. Only three months after the Bastille fell, he wrote Lafayette, "I dread the reveries of your philosophic politicians." Jefferson, who was on the spot as our ambassador to France, was hopeful, and would remain so for the next six or seven years. "I have never feared for the ultimate result," he wrote Lafayette in April 1790 after he had returned home. Thomas Paine was the most enthusiastic founder of all. In 1792 he was given honorary French citizenship and elected to the national legislature, even though he could hardly speak French.

In the short run, the skeptics were right. The French Revolution brought ten years of violence and corruption: Paine just missed being guillotined. It was followed, in the founders' lifetime, by Napoleon and two royal dynasties. Gouverneur Morris, who succeeded Jefferson as our ambassador to France and lived in Paris during the Reign of Terror, thought France was "like a vicious horse." It "may kick and plunge, but the whip and spur well applied will tame her." This is the anthropological view of liberty, and democracy: the rights of men vary according to where men live. Yet the most stable regimes in France's modern history have been two republics, the Third (1871–1940) and the Fifth (1958–ongoing). If even France has had some success with democracy, perhaps other nations can as well.

What Did the Founders Think of Pacifism?

Quakers were one of the largest sects in colonial America (in 1750, only Congregationalists and Anglicans had more houses of worship). Benjamin Franklin spent much of his adult life in Philadelphia, which they had founded.

As a young journalist, he engaged in polemics against Quakers who were unwilling to defend the colony during the French and Indian Wars, since that would involve them in war making. Shouldn't "they who are against fortifying their country against an enemy," he asked, also "be against shutting and locking their doors at night?" In practice, he found that many Quakers were

willing to support self-defense, so long as they could do so indi-
rectly (voting money "for the King's use," without specifying that
it would be spent on the military, or paying for "grain," without
saying that the grains would be gunpowder). Quaker purists were
roughly treated by the State of Pennsylvania during the Revolu-.
tion. The state government required all voters to swear loyalty
oaths, which Quakers could not do; Quaker leaders were arrested
on bogus charges of corresponding with the enemy and deported
to western Virginia.

After signing the Peace of Paris in 1783, Franklin wrote an old
English friend and fellow scientist, Sir Joseph Banks. "I hope it
will be lasting, and that mankind will at length, as they call themselves reasonable creatures, have reason and sense enough to settle their differences without cutting throats; for in my opinion,
there never was a good war, or a bad peace." Franklin showed his
usual gift for expressing the mood of the moment. He could
afford to be pacific; he had just won.

Would the Founders Fear an American Empire?

The fear that America has traded its republican character for an
imperial one is a common one, taken up by critics Left and Right
whenever the United States is pursuing a foreign policy with
which they disagree. It was most memorably expressed in 1924 by
Robinson Jeffers, in his poem "Shine, Perishing Republic." "This
America settles in the mold of its vulgarity, heavily thickening to
empire . . . "

Emperors were devil figures in the historical imagination of
the founders. The worst insult they could call each other was
Caesar, meaning either Julius or his grand-nephew Augustus, the
betrayers of the Roman Republic. Thomas Jefferson claimed that

Alexander Hamilton told him over dinner that Julius Caesar was "the greatest man that ever lived." (Jefferson added piously that his favorite great men were Isaac Newton, Francis Bacon, and John Locke.) Hamilton, for his part, reminded George Washington that Caesar was a demagogue, and so was Jefferson. The younger founders had a modern Caesar before their very eyes in the person of Napoleon Bonaparte, the republican general who became first consul, consul for life, and finally emperor of France. Hamilton compared Aaron Burr to Bonaparte. Jefferson compared Bonaparte to Hamilton. John Adams said that Hamilton was a cut-rate, West Indian Bonaparte. Putting a crown on one's head was the greatest political infamy the founders could imagine; the greatest political virtue, exemplified in their own ranks by Washington, was to refuse all such temptations.

But empires do not have to have emperors. An empire could be an imperial extent of territory. This was something the founders predicted and desired for the United States. The phrase "this rising empire" tolls through Washington's letters and speeches for decades, like a bell. When he talked his unpaid officers out of mutinying at Newburgh, New York, in the last days of the Revolution, he urged them not to "deluge our rising Empire in blood." The first paragraph of the first *Federalist* paper, written by Hamilton, promises that the series will discuss "the fate of an empire, in many respects the most interesting in the world." One month after James Madison took office as president, Jefferson dropped him a letter from Monticello, surveying the international scene and setting the limits for future American expansion. Jefferson's idea of America's limits was more expansive than anything America ever achieved, for he expected us to acquire Cuba and Canada. Then, he wrote, "we should have such an empire for liberty as she has never surveyed since the creation: and I am persuaded no constitution was ever before so well calculated as ours for extensive empire and self government."

If a republic would not disappear simply by reaching the size of an empire, it could falter by acquiring imperial institutions. Jefferson was ever suspicious of what he considered these to be— banks, standing armies—though his fears had the effect of undermining his confident predictions. Because the United States had no professional soldiers, and no funds with which to pay any, the War of 1812, in which he confidently expected to acquire Canada—"We . . . have only to include the North in our confederacy," he wrote in his letter to Madison, "which would be of course in the first war"—ended in a draw. Jefferson and his peers quarreled about ways and means, timing and tempo, but none doubted that America could be an empire and a republic at the same time.

Almost none doubted it. John Adams, who believed in cycles of history, expected America to go down into vice, even as it rose up in freedom. After the Revolutionary War, he lectured his fellow diplomat Jefferson that "neither philosophy, nor religion, nor morality, nor wisdom, nor interest, will ever govern nations or parties, against their vanity, their pride . . . their avarice or ambition." At that moment (1787) he foresaw the wars that would not end until the Battle of Waterloo in 1815. The conflict, Adams predicted, "will render our country, whether she is forced into it, or not, rich, great and powerful in comparison [to] what she now is." He was right; the long Anglo-French war would give us Louisiana, and get Britain finally off our backs. But this, Adams thought, was not a good thing, for success would corrupt. "Riches, grandeur and power will have the same effect upon American as [they have] upon European minds. . . . A Covent Garden rake will never be wise enough to take warning from the claps caught by his companions." Only bad experience could bring renewal and start the cycle again. "When he comes to be poxed himself, he may possibly repent and reform."

Adams was always contrary, especially with himself. Twenty-five years later, he welcomed the War of 1812, and fretted that Jefferson had not kept the American navy strong enough.

CHAPTER 7

Education and Media

SINCE the founders meant America to be a republic, Americans would have to be able to understand questions of law, money, and war. Fortunately, the founders were living in a knowledge explosion: America had nine colleges and twenty-five newspapers in 1776, serving a population of 2.5 million. (That compares to more than forty-one hundred colleges and fourteen hundred newspapers, in a country of almost 300 million today. Colleges have zoomed past the rate of increase of population, though newspapers have fallen behind.) Benjamin Franklin, whose activities as a printer and a journalist were partly responsible for the explosion, testified that "reading became fashionable" in America in the 1730s. Since Americans had "no publick amusements to divert their attention from study," they soon became "better instructed and more intelligent" than people in other countries.

The founders were passionately concerned with instructing their peers, and their children. The intelligence they wanted to develop was political and practical. As John Adams made his way to Philadelphia for the first Continental Congress in 1774, his thoughts turned to the children he had left behind in Braintree. "Fix their ambition," he wrote his wife, "upon great and solid objects, and their contempt upon little, frivolous and useless ones." The people would shape America; their children would shape the future.

What Would the Founders Have Thought about Tuition Tax Credits or Private-School Vouchers?

The founders encouraged both private and public education (one of their plans for public education was more ambitious than anything America has ever done). They worried less about who paid for education and who ran it than the end result: well-informed citizens who could sustain a republic.

Their interest in education was not correlated with the amount they had. Alexander Hamilton never graduated from King's College in New York City, since he left to become a captain of artillery in the Revolution. But later in life he served as a trustee of King's, renamed Columbia, and of the Oneida Academy, a school for Indians in upstate New York, which gratefully took his name (Hamilton College). George Washington never even went to college, but he gave money to colleges in Maryland and Virginia (now Washington College and Washington and Lee University). Benjamin Franklin missed college too, but he founded a school that ultimately became one (now the University of Pennsylvania). Men often "catch . . . a taste for cultivating flowers," he wrote, touting his brainchild, so why not "a relish for [the] culture of young minds?"

All these schools were private ventures, but some of the founders had grander plans. In 1779 Jefferson wrote the Bill for the Diffusion of General Knowledge in the state of Virginia. He envisioned a pyramidal system based on a network of neighborhood primary schools, followed by grammar schools each serving several counties, culminating in the College of William and Mary, his alma mater. The public would support the primary schools, while private funding would help pay for the higher levels. Jefferson wanted some education for everyone, and a lot of education for the talented, and he wanted it for political reasons. Since even "the best forms" of government tended to revert to tyranny over time, "the people at large" had to have enough knowledge of history "to know ambition under all its shapes"; the most talented people needed additional training, to enable them "to guard the sacred deposit" of liberty.

The legislature balked. Jefferson's plan seemed expensive, and it was not clear how a network of lower schools could be established in a vast rural state with a low population density. Jefferson continued to push for his plan anyway. In 1786, he wrote his old teacher George Wythe from Paris. He loved the French, he said, yet their oppressive political and religious institutions made them wretched. "Let our countrymen know, that the people alone can protect us against these evils, and that the tax which will be paid for this purpose, is not more than the thousandth part of what will be paid to kings, priests and nobles, who will rise up among us if we leave the people in ignorance."

Virginia continued to dawdle. Kings, priests, and nobles did not rise up there, but Jefferson at the end of his life devised a new plan: a state university (he no longer trusted William and Mary to fill the role). In 1818 he wrote a report to the legislature, with James Madison's help, in which he listed the "objects" of the proposed institution. Once again, politics was uppermost in his mind: the university should "form the statesmen, legislators and judges, on whom public prosperity and individual happiness are so much to depend," and "expound the principles and structure of government" that "shall leave us free to do whatever does not violate the equal rights of another." Other goals followed, but politics led the list. Jefferson worked on the University of Virginia for the rest of his life, designing the buildings, hiring the professors, overseeing the curriculum, and pressuring Madison and James Monroe to serve as visitors, or trustees (he pressured them by assuming that they would be as enthusiastic as he was). Founding the University of Virginia is one of the three achievements he wanted inscribed on his tombstone, along with writing the statute of Virginia for religious freedom and the Declaration. Education was Jefferson's religion, and the foundation of independence.

The University of Virginia was meant to serve the state. Washington had a plan that was grander yet. In his first annual message to Congress (we now call it the State of the Union address) he told his audience that "nothing . . . can better deserve your patronage" than education. His reasons, like Jefferson's, were political. He wanted people to "value their own rights"; he also wanted them to be able to acknowledge "the necessary exercise of lawful authority" (the former general was always mindful of the question of command). He left it to Congress to decide whether to subsidize existing "seminaries of learning" or to establish a new "national university." This was a bold idea indeed. Britain had universities that were hundreds of years old—several of the founders had attended them—but not an institution for the whole nation. Washington felt that a small, ambitious country—a rising empire—was especially in need of one.

He was still pushing the idea in his eighth and last message to Congress. Now he was certain that America needed a brand-new school. "Our country, much to its honor, contains many seminaries of learning highly respectable and useful; but the funds upon which they rest are too narrow to command the ablest professors." He wanted a national university to make young Americans "more homogenous" in "principles, opinions and manners." He also wanted the university to specialize in the "science of government." "In a republic, what species of knowledge can be equally important?"

Every founder who became president endorsed a national university (for example, President Madison, who said it would spread "national feelings, "liberal sentiments," and "congenial manners"). None of the Congresses populated by founders would set one up. Executives had a vision, but legislators were mindful of difficulties and costs, as well as jealousies—where, in a sprawling country, would such an institution be? America has had to acquire its knowledge and its nationalism on an ad hoc basis.

What Would the Founders Put in the Curriculum?

It was fine to want knowledge. But what knowledge would the founders get?

Benjamin Franklin took up the question of curriculums in the 1749 prospectus he wrote for the academy that ultimately became the University of Pennsylvania. He clothed himself in educational authorities—John Milton, John Locke—but his curriculum was unusual for the mid-eighteenth century.

Franklin's central subject was history. "As nothing teaches (saith Mr. Locke) so nothing delights more than HISTORY." He was always tugging it in practical directions, however—applying it to the present, or using it to teach a skill. History showed the power of oratory that, in modern times, was "chiefly performed by the pen and press"; in other words, Franklin's students would study journalism as well as rhetoric. In studying history, "questions of right and wrong" would "naturally arise." Students should debate them. "Publick disputes warm the imagination, whet the industry, and strengthen the natural abilities." Franklin also wanted students to be instructed in gardening, mechanics, drawing, and swimming. "'Tis some advantage . . . to be free from the slavish terrors" nonswimmers feel "when they are obliged to be on the water even in crossing a ferry." Franklin included religion as a historical and civic subject: "History will . . . afford frequent opportunities of showing the necessity of a publick religion . . . and the excellency of the CHRISTIAN RELIGION above all others ancient or modern." Christianity was worth studying because it was as useful as swimming.

An eighteenth-century reader would have noticed what was missing from Franklin's list: Greek and Latin, then the mainstays of education (Jefferson, expressing the conventional view, would later testify that he would not exchange his knowledge of Greek and Latin for any other subjects he might have learned instead). Franklin slyly justified the omission by citing the Roman author Pliny. "In his letter to a lady on chusing a tutor for her son . . . he does not advise her to a Greek master of rhetoric, tho' the Greeks were famous for that science; but to a Latin master, because Latin was the boy's mother tongue." If Franklin had prevailed, then all the younger founding journalists, from Publius on down, would have had to look elsewhere for their pseudonyms.

Franklin's educational ideas must have had some merit, for the first graduating class of the academy—seven boys—included two future founders: Francis Hopkinson, who would sign the Declaration, and Hugh Williamson, who would sign the Constitution. In a few years, however, Franklin lost control of the institution, and its curriculum reverted to more traditional channels, including the classics. One of the graduates of this regimen would be the Constitution's draftsman, Gouverneur Morris.

Two of the founders were college presidents, and had to face the question of curriculums very concretely. In 1768 the Reverend John Witherspoon, a Presbyterian minister in Edinburgh, crossed the Atlantic with his wife, five children, and three hundred books in order to take charge of the College of New Jersey at Princeton. Like all college presidents then and since, he spent much of his time raising money. He taught courses in moral philosophy, history, eloquence, and divinity, as well as French and Hebrew in a pinch. Witherspoon hacked at the question of epistemology—how do we know what we know? He added a moral sense to the five physical ones: "It is the law which our Maker has written upon our hearts . . . enforce[ing] duty, previous to all reasoning." Sometimes it counseled revolution. "In experience, there are many instances of rulers becoming tyrants, but . . . very few causeless and premature rebellions." Witherspoon's moral sense led him to the Continental Congress, where he signed the Declaration; his students included James Madison, who suffered a breakdown from working too hard, and Aaron Burr.

William Samuel Johnson was the first president of Columbia when the college was renamed and reopened after the Revolution. Johnson was not as venturesome as Witherspoon politically—he had sat out the Revolution as a neutral—but he embraced the new American order (Connecticut tapped him to be a delegate to the Constitutional Convention, and one of its first two senators). Johnson was a little too venturesome academically. He hired Johann Christoph Kunze, a German minister, to teach Oriental languages: Hebrew, Syriac, Aramaic, and Arabic. No one wanted to learn these subjects, so the position was terminated after a few years. He also hired James Kent, a brilliant young lawyer friend of Alexander Hamilton, to lecture on law. That job also withered from lack of interest (twenty years later, Kent's *Commentaries on American Law* became a standard legal reference). If Johnson had less impact than Witherspoon, it was not from lack of trying.

Jefferson in old age gave copious thought to the curriculum of the University of Virginia, but perhaps the most interesting academic advice he ever gave was in 1786 to his nephew Peter Carr, who had just entered William and Mary to study with George Wythe. Jefferson sent Carr a list of subjects and books, but emphasized a few points in a covering letter. Traveling, the perk of education from the grand tour to junior year abroad, was not what it was cracked up to be; it "makes men wiser, but less happy." (Jefferson issued this criticism of travel from Paris.) Italian was one modern language too many; better for Carr to study Spanish, since "our future connections with . . . Spanish America will render that language a valuable acquisition." Jefferson agreed with Witherspoon on the existence of an innate moral sense—so much so that he told Carr to skip moral philosophy altogether. "State a moral case to a ploughman and a professor. The former will decide it as well, and often better than the latter, because he has not been led astray by artificial rules."

Most important, Carr was now old enough to examine religion. "Fix reason firmly in her seat," his uncle told him, and question everything. "Do not be frightened from this inquiry by any fear of its consequences. If it ends in a belief that there is no God, you will find incitements to virtue in the comfort and pleasantness" of being virtuous. "If you find reason to believe there is a God," you will be inspired by "the consciousness that you are acting under his eye." If there is an afterlife, "the hope of a happy existence . . . increases the appetite to deserve it." If Jesus was a God, "you will be comforted by a belief [in] his aid and love." Jefferson concluded, "Your own reason is the only oracle given you by heaven." Even if there is no heaven? Reason and virtue were Jefferson's heaven. He never expressed this advice in a curriculum, but he shared it with his nearest and dearest.

Would the Founders Teach Intelligent Design?

A few of the founders were doctors, and Thomas Jefferson was a gentleman student of scientific subjects—animals, fossils, Indian languages—but the only founder who was a true scientist was Benjamin Franklin. It is a delight to look over his shoulder and watch his mind at work. In the corners of a busy life, with the simplest equipment, he performed experiments not only on his signature subject, lightning, which earned him Kant's compliment as "the new Prometheus," but also on heat and colors, oil and water, evaporation, hydraulics, and marsh gas. He was curious, clever, and provisional; he was not wedded to old theories: "A new appearance [phenomenon], if it cannot be explain'd by our old principles, may afford us new ones, of use perhaps in explaining some other obscure parts of natural knowledge." Nor was he unduly proud of his own efforts: "It may be of use to relate the circumstances even of an experiment that does not succeed, since they may give hints of amendment in future trials: it is therefore I have been thus particular." He knew that science was a collective enterprise, pursued by researchers confirming or correcting each other's observations, which is why he cherished his memberships in scientific societies around the world. Franklin being Franklin, he also mocked science, with an insider's perfect pitch, as in his spoof proposal to the Royal Academy of Brussels that they discover "some drug wholesome & not disagreeable" that would make farts smell like perfume.

One subject Franklin stopped examining after he was a young man was the study of first causes, or metaphysics. "The great uncertainty I found in metaphysical reasonings disgusted me," Franklin wrote when he was in his seventies, "and I quitted that kind of reading and study for others more satisfactory." Some of the founders shared Franklin's bafflement with metaphysical reasonings (John Adams played with philosophical skepticism; Jefferson clung, rather uneasily, to the evidence of his five, or six, senses)—an odd reluctance, since metaphysical reasonings might shed light on important political questions, such as the worth of mankind. The founders instead took the rights of man as a given, or as a discovery of an independent branch of science: "The rights of mankind," George Washington wrote, "were better understood and more clearly defined" at the end of the eighteenth century, thanks to the "researches" of "philosophers, sages and legislatures, through a long succession of years." Sages and legislators were the political equivalents of experimenters like Franklin.

The founders also looked for the rights of man in religion. In the Declaration, Jefferson appealed, in words as stirring as they were unlocalized, to "the laws of nature and of nature's God." Dr. Benjamin Rush, who signed the Declaration, looked specifically to "the religion of JESUS CHRIST." In a 1786 essay on republican education, Rush wrote that the Genesis account of the creation of man was "the best refutation that can be given to the divine right of kings," and "the strongest argument . . . in favor of the original and natural equality of all mankind." If we are all descended from Adam, then none of us can claim to belong to a higher order of beings. Not everyone who read Genesis found the same things in it. Sir Robert Filmer, a seventeenth-century essayist, claimed that Adam's "lordship . . . over the whole world" was inherited by kings. Filmer's arguments were popular enough that John Locke spent many pages refuting them, and they lasted long enough that Tories were still recycling them during the American Revolution. Religious reasonings were as contentious as metaphysical ones; still some founders invoked them.

The founders kept their categories clear. Even when they drew a blank, they knew what they were thinking about. They would not have smuggled metaphysics into science, or appealed to natural science to judge questions of religion or human rights. Their design of the branches of knowledge was more intelligent than ours often is.

Would the Founders Allow Journalists to Protect Their Sources?

One founder, who was a source, went to extraordinary lengths to protect his own source. In June 1773 an explosive story appeared in the *Boston Gazette*. It printed letters of advice that Thomas Hutchinson, a colonial official, had sent London about how to pacify the restless colony. He did not counsel kindness: Hutchinson wrote, "There must be an abridgement of what are called English liberties." Here was confirmation of the Bostonians' worst fears. British heavy-handedness was not due to ignorance or inattention; it was the fate their imperial masters intended for

WHAT WOULD THE FOUNDERS DO?

them. If there was a story that made the Revolution inevitable, this was it.

How had the *Gazette* gotten its scoop? Someone in power must have leaked the letters, and everyone in London wanted to know who. Rumors identified this or that person; two possible sources fought a duel, each protesting his innocence. To prevent further bloodshed, the culprit stepped forward himself. On Christmas 1773 Benjamin Franklin placed a notice in a London newspaper saying that he was Deep Throat.

The sixty-eight-year-old Franklin had been living the life of an expat London insider for the past nine years. He was the lobbyist for four American colonies, and the deputy postmaster general for all of North America; his son William was royal governor of New Jersey. Franklin's intentions in spilling the beans were not the same as the *Boston Gazette*'s. Franklin still believed that the British Empire could benefit both England and its colonies. He sent the Hutchinson letters to Massachusetts for the information of a few local leaders only, to show them that their troubles came from an overzealous local official. The *Boston Gazette* printed them in a different spirit, to show the rottenness of the whole system. Franklin, who had been involved in journalism since he was a teenager, surely ought to have known that newspapers love leaks, and love to put their own spin on them. Now he tried to limit the damage; he would not say who had given the letters to him.

The British government wanted to know. Franklin was summoned before a committee of the Privy Council, the king's intimate advisers, in January 1774. For one hour, Solicitor General Alexander Wedderburn abused him as a common thief. "I hope, my lords, you will mark and brand this man, for the honour of this country, of Europe, and of mankind. . . . Men will watch him with a jealous eye; they will hide their papers from him and lock up their escritoires [writing desks]. He will henceforth esteem it a libel to be called"—here Wedderburn made a joke—"a man of letters." Franklin took it in silence. The next day he learned he had been fired from his post office job.

Franklin's ordeal showed him that there was no good in the empire: the men who ran it, from Boston to London, were narrow-minded and implacable. The experience certainly showed him that there was no longer any good in the empire for Benjamin Franklin. He returned home to Philadelphia the following year, and was elected to the second Continental Congress.

What strikes us today about Franklin's ordeal is its mildness. His letters were opened, and he lost his job, but he was not arrested; no one ransacked his house. Oppressive governments usually oppress more seriously. Franklin took the secret of his source to his grave. There was no old-age tell-all, no posthumous revelation. Historians guess, but 233 years later we still don't know who his Deep Throat was.

When the founders set up a government of their own, it leaked like a sieve. George Washington's secretary of state, Thomas Jefferson, planted antiadministration stories in the *National Gazette* of Philadelphia. Alexander Hamilton, the treasury secretary, defended his policies in another Philadelphia paper, the *Gazette of the United States*. Washington asked his advisers to stop their polemics, but did not fire them. When founders were seriously displeased with journalists, they did not hunt after leaks, but took more drastic measures (see the sections on objective journalism below, and censorship in liberty and law, above).

Did the Founders Believe in Objective Journalism?

The founders kept the press in its place. No journalists covered the Constitutional Convention; one of the few times that George Washington, the presiding officer, spoke was to chide an unknown delegate for having left his copy of the minutes lying about. "I must entreat Gentlemen to be more careful," Washington said, "lest our transactions get into the newspapers, and disturb the public repose by premature speculations." Neither Washington nor any other founding president submitted to anything like a press conference. When President Washington wished to communicate something, he would consult his cabinet or give a formal speech to Congress; when President Jefferson wished to communicate something, he would send a written address to Congress or hold an intimate dinner at the White House. Whatever the founders thought about the creation of man in Genesis, they considered professional journalists—that is, those who did nothing else for a living—to be a lower order of being. No gentleman ever dueled a journalist; in a pinch, your friends might beat one up for you.

Yet, though the founders kept journalism in its place, they chose to occupy a large place in it. Samuel Adams and Benjamin Franklin published newspapers; Alexander Hamilton founded one, the *New-York Evening Post*, that is still being published. All three wrote copiously for their own and other newspapers. Other founders who joined them in freelancing included John Adams, John Dickinson, John Jay, Rufus King, Richard Henry Lee, Robert Livingston, James Madison, James Monroe, and Edmund Randolph. If they didn't write themselves, they got other people to write for them. When Jefferson was secretary of state, he hired Philip Freneau, a college classmate of James Madison, to work as a government translator, though Freneau's real job was to edit the *National Gazette*, a newspaper that attacked policies and personnel of the Washington administration that Jefferson disliked. When Vice President Adams came in for criticism (from Jefferson, among others), he was defended in the *Columbian Centinel* by a writer using the name "Publicola." Most readers assumed "Publicola" was Adams himself, which he denied. Adams was telling the truth—barely, for "Publicola" was actually his son, John Quincy Adams. Pseudonyms facilitated these subterfuges, while they encouraged political junkies to guess the real author, even as they try to guess leakers today.

The founders wrote hard because the country was new: they were writing the script, and if the project stalled they had to rewrite. Another spur to their productivity was the fact that the country was a republic. Lawmakers were chosen by voters, and constrained by public opinion. Like clever and combative intellectuals in every age, the founders sometimes enjoyed pushing each other's buttons, playing games of theoretical one-upmanship, but they knew that if they provoked America, they would not be allowed to found it. At the Constitutional Convention, Hamilton toyed with abolishing state governments. "Great economy might be obtained," the future treasury secretary observed. But he immediately added that he was only kidding. "He did not mean however to shock the public opinion by proposing such a measure." When the people had such power, it was necessary to inform, persuade, and inspire them. Despots faced no such burdens. Frederick the Great could rally his troops by asking, "Do you dogs want to live forever?" Leaders in a republic had to take their time. The founders' obsession with journalism was an extension of their concern for education.

That did not mean that they imagined the press would or

should be objective. They wrote as partisans, and they expected the newspapers they read to do the same. The first editor of the *New-York Evening Post*, picked by Hamilton, was a lawyer-journalist named William Coleman. Coleman once described how editorials in the *Post* got written: "[Hamilton] appoints a time when I may see him. . . . [A]s soon as I see him he begins in a deliberate manner to dictate and I to note down in shorthand; when he stops my article is completed." No press lord has ever done it more directly, though Hamilton knew more than most press lords.

There were degrees of partisanship. American newspapers of the founding era were full of lies, but this was thought to be in bad taste. "I have sometimes, indeed, suspected," wrote Franklin in a censorious mood, "that those papers are the manufacture of foreign enemies" who wished to make America "appear contemptible and detestable all the world over." Franklin, of course, had committed many deceptions to print, from revolutionary propaganda to hoaxes, like the "Speech of Miss Polly Baker," supposedly delivered in a Connecticut courtroom by a woman charged with bearing her fifth illegitimate child. "How can it be believed," Polly asked the judges, "that Heaven is angry at my having children, when to the little done by me towards it, God has been pleased to add his divine skill and admirable workmanship in the formation of their bodies, and crown'd it by furnishing them with rational and immortal souls?" The fact that Polly never existed did not prevent her speech from being reprinted numerous times as truth. Nevertheless, honesty was valued as a rhetorical technique, which was why the founders, when they did not pretend to be ancient Romans, sometimes chose pseudonyms (Common Sense, A Plain Honest Man) that stressed their candor. "My arguments," wrote Hamilton in the first *Federalist* paper, "will be open to all and may be judged of by all." The highest art of journalism is artlessness.

Even if the founders confined themselves to the truth, they gave relentlessly one-sided accounts of it. Their journalism was polemical; they specialized in op-eds. They could be brilliant, eloquent, or wise; a modern columnist can only look at the *Federalist Papers*, each two thousand words long, written at a rate of four or more a week, and shake his head. But the founders were always partisan. The stakes were simply too high to shirk the burden of deciding.

After the election of 1800, Gouverneur Morris wrote Robert Livingston: "My dear friend, this farce of life contains nothing which should put us out of humor." The election of 1800, deadlocked in the electoral college and decided by the House of Representatives, was the most acrid the founders knew; Morris, who was serving as senator at the time, had a ringside seat on the final crisis. His lightheartedness, so characteristic of him, was most uncharacteristic of the other founders (it was the main reason so many of them considered Morris an oddball). Life was not a farce to them, but a drama, in which they and the American people, their readers, all had major parts. Morris's friend Hamilton spoke for the founding journalists when he said, "I condemn those indifferent mortals, who either never form opinions, or never make them known."

CHAPTER 8

Men and Women

$\mathscr{D}$ID WOMEN have to go to school and follow the news along with men? Would America profit from their accomplishments, or suffer from the limitations placed upon them?

The founders believed the sexes were different, certainly as far as public life was concerned. Men and women could not play the same roles in war, politics, or talking about war and politics. "There are certain appropriate duties assigned to each sex," wrote one of the earliest historians of the founding. It was "the more peculiar province of masculine strength" both "to repel the bold invader of the rights of his country" and "to describe the blood-stained field . . . in the nervous style of manly eloquence."

The historian who wrote those words was Mercy Otis Warren, sister of one founder, James Otis, and wife of another, James Warren. Mrs. Warren, who was a successful playwright before the

Revolution, turned to history after it because she believed that "a concern for the welfare of society ought equally to glow in every human breast"—male or female. She might not describe the blood-stained field firsthand, but she could write about her country.

Women had fewer rights in the founding period than they do now, but they were not without responsibilities and influence.

Did the Founders Think Women Were as Smart as Men?

Almost no women voted during the founding period (as discussed later), yet the founders did talk politics with women. If they did not allow smart women to be their peers, they treated them as intelligent onlookers.

John Adams's political sounding board was his wife, Abigail. Much of their famous correspondence was about current events. During the Battle of Bunker Hill, Abigail was closer to the fighting than John ever got (she could hear the cannon, and see the smoke, from their house in Braintree). Her comments on public figures are shrewd, and pointed: "Poor Gerry," she said of Elbridge Gerry, whom she liked, "always had a wrong kink in his head." Abigail Adams had her own kinks. Brilliant as John, she was also as temperamental, and could act as an echo chamber for his worst qualities—rage, resentment, paranoia. During the crisis over the Sedition Act, she railed at newspaper editors who attacked her husband president. "In any other country," they "would have been seized long ago." Abigail Adams proved that men and women were equally capable of bad judgment.

Gouverneur Morris discussed politics with one of his lovers. From 1789 to 1795 he lived in France, and watched the French Revolution unfold. His fellow spectator and mistress for much of that time was Adelaide de Flahaut, the pretty young wife of an old count. Mme. de Flahaut was a successful novelist—she named a minor character in one of her books "Dr. Morris"—and the hostess of a popular salon, a weekly gathering of intellectual socialites. A frequent guest was her other lover, Talleyrand, a Catholic bishop and politician who played a prominent role in the Revolution's early liberal phase. She and Morris hoped Talleyrand would become Louis XVI's reforming chief minister, and two months after the Bastille fell they drew up lists of men who should serve in his government. "Then, my friend," Mme. de Flahaut told Morris, "you and I will govern France." "The kingdom," Morris observed in his diary, "is actually in much worse hands." Their hopes came to nothing; no amount of good advice could save the French Revolution.

George Washington got better advice from Mrs. Eliza Powel, a Philadelphia hostess. Mrs. Powel liked being in the know—it was she who asked Benjamin Franklin, after the Constitutional Convention ended, what sort of government the delegates had devised, prompting his immortal quip, "A republic, if you can keep it." That was high-level chitchat, the stuff of Georgetown dinner parties (if they have guests as quick as this eighteenth-century pair). In the fall of 1792 she gave Washington something more significant—a piece of her mind.

Washington had been telling his inner circle for months that he planned to retire at the end of his first term. He was sixty years old; he had been commander in chief for eight and a half years, president for almost four; his cabinet was riven by tiresome feuds. All his male advisers were horrified by this plan; the structure of the new Constitution seemed too flimsy to survive if Washington bailed out. James Madison expressed "anxious wishes and hopes" that he would stay on; Alexander Hamilton said it would be "the greatest evil that could befall the country" if he didn't. Still Washington yearned for home.

By November the presidential balloting was under way. Washington was sure to win—he had no opponents—but he could still decline to serve. Mrs. Powel swung into action. She wrote her good friend the president a letter making three arguments. The country needed him: "The repose of millions" depended on his serving a second term. His character required it of him: "You have frequently demonstrated that you possess an empire over yourself. For God's sake, do not yield that empire to a love of ease." His reputation required it of him: if he retired now, people would say that he had left office because it "promised nothing [more] to your ambition," and "might eventually involve your popularity." At first blush, arguments two and three could be dismissed as traditional "women's" concerns: the personal masquerading as the political. But in late-eighteenth-century America the political subsumed the personal: the founders, more than any generation before or since, had made themselves into public figures. They lived on the stage of history, where they pledged their lives, fortunes, and sacred honor to the freedom and happiness of their country. Mrs. Powel was calling in Washington's pledge. She could take no direct part in politics, but she could frankly hold the father of his country to the part he had written for himself. Abigail Adams was married to power, and Adelaide de Flahaut slept with it—traditional conduits for women's advice in societies that do not let them vote or hold office. Mrs. Powel was offering advice, not to an equal—no one was Washington's equal—but to a friend, and fellow citizen.

There is no answering letter in her papers, and no copy of one in Washington's, so if he replied it must have been in person. Washington accepted his reelection, which, like his first election, was unanimous. The strongest factor in his decision was no doubt his own sense of duty, but Mrs. Powel's letter had helped frame the issues.

Would the Founders Believe in Equal Rights?

The most famous letter Abigail Adams sent John was on March 31, 1776.

> I long to hear that you have declared an independency—and by the way in the new code of laws which I suppose it will be necessary for you to make I desire you would remember the ladies, and be more generous and favourable to them than your ancestors. . . . If perticuliar care and attention is not paid to the laidies, we are determined to foment a rebelion, and will not hold ourselves bound by any laws in which we have not voice, or representation.

She wrote this partly in jest, and John replied wholly so. "We know better than to repeal our masculine systems. . . . We have only the name of masters, and rather than give up this, which would completely subject us to the despotism of the peticoat, I hope General Washington, and all our brave heroes would fight."

Abigail wrote a more serious letter on August 14. "If we mean to have heroes, statesmen and philosophers, we should have learned women. . . . If much depends as is allowed upon the early education of youth and the first principals which are instilld take the deepest root, great benifit must arise from litirary accomplishments in women."

This was a poignant appeal, given her history. In the eighteenth century smart girls in wealthy families were sometimes taught at home. The Reverend William Smith taught his daughter Abigail Milton and Shakespeare. Mercy Otis shared her brother James's studies before and after he went to Harvard. No girls, however, could go to Harvard, or any other school. One consequence of Abigail Adams's home schooling was that her spelling—*perticuliar, principals, benifit, litirary*—was erratic, even by the more freewheeling norms of the eighteenth century. Abigail would have blossomed with schooling, as a plant soaks up water. She did the best with what she had, for herself and her children. Her only daughter married badly, and two of her sons became drunks, but the other son, John Quincy Adams, became president. Good first principles benefited him.

Abigail's belief in the political importance of educating women was shared by other founders. In the winter of 1792 Senator Aaron Burr was in Philadelphia, the nation's capital, absorbed in a new book, Mary Wollstonecraft's *Vindication of the Rights of Women*. "In order to spread those enlightening principles, which alone can meliorate the fate of man, women must be allowed to found their virtue on knowledge," Wollstonecraft declared. Burr sent an enthusiastic review of the book to his wife, Theodosia, back in New York. "As I read with avidity and prepossession everything written by a lady, I made haste to procure it, and spent the last night, almost the whole of it, in reading it. . . . I promise myself much pleasure in reading it to you." In Burr's writing seriousness and levity chase each other like squirrels. But he was serious enough about women's education to see that his daughter, also named Theodosia, was given an exacting one, learning ancient authors like Terence and Horace, and contemporary ones like Edward Gibbon, as well as piano, ballet, and skating. By the time she turned seventeen, he was satisfied with the result. "You reflect, and that is a security for your conduct." (No one ever said that of her father.)

Abigail Adams hoped that education would benefit American women in their roles as mothers and wives, not as political actors in their own right. There was one place in late-eighteenth-century America, however (which was also the only place in the world), where women voted. On July 2, 1776, two days before the Declaration of Independence, the first revolutionary constitution of the State of New Jersey gave the vote not to "freemen," the language used in other states, but to "inhabitants." There was a property qualification: New Jersey's voting "inhabitants" had to be worth fifty pounds (perhaps twenty-five hundred dollars today). Since family property was in the husband's name, married women were automatically excluded. But widows and single women might make the cut. At the time no one commented on the change of language, and its implications. Most likely it was an inadvertence: the New Jersey Constitution had been cobbled together in a few days, since the state was on the verge of invasion and civil war. But women noticed the loophole, and so did politicians. After the war New Jersey laws regulating elections began to include language specifying what the voter should do with his or her ballot.

This was an astonishing development. The eighteenth century was a great age of theorizing and daydreaming. Rousseau wrote a constitution for the kingdom of Poland as well as a novel describing how children should be raised. Poland never used the one, and educators only slowly absorbed the lessons of the other. But in America, in a state that was middling in every way—size, location, political luster—people were effecting a revolutionary change.

The end came in 1807, in the name of reform. That year

Essex County held a special election to decide whether the county courthouse should remain in Newark or move to Elizabeth. All politics is local, as Tip O'Neill said, and the location of the courthouse was a hot topic. The vote was crooked even by New Jersey standards (one township with three hundred legal voters cast eighteen hundred votes). In a spasm of morality, the state legislature decided to purge the voting rolls, and restricted the franchise to white male adults (New Jersey politics did not noticeably improve even so). Women would not vote again in America, or anywhere else, until 1869, when the territory of Wyoming let them back to the polls.

Radical as it was, New Jersey's founding experience of woman suffrage was an exercise in opportunism rather than idealism. It does not prove that even a minority of founders thought that all men and women were created equal. At most it proves a negative: when a woman's right to vote was granted fortuitously, it did not strike New Jersey's founders as so unseemly that it should be immediately revoked, as a law converting New Jersey (or any other state) into a monarchy would have been. The founders knew what they thought about kings (and queens). They were less certain when it came to women—so much less that they let some women vote for thirty-one years. Opportunism can accomplish a lot, though its gains have to be nailed down by principle.

What Did the Founders Think of Women in the Workforce?

Some founding-era women pursued careers outside the home, and some founders took note of them. Mercy Otis Warren, besides being the sister and wife of founders, was a longtime friend of the Adamses. They recognized, in her tart, ardent mind a kindred spirit. As she researched her history of the Revolution she pumped John for information about his activities as a diplomat. Adams wrote back that he had been an effective, though unconventional, negotiator. "You should immortalize my imprudence," he boasted. She immortalized him, all right, claiming that his years of service at European courts had seduced him from republican virtue. When Adams read that, he sent her no less than ten rebuttals, which she, in reply, called "rambling . . . angry . . . undigested . . . captious, malignant, irrelevant." Adams raged because he felt betrayed by a friend and, worse, by a friend whose opinions he respected.

Sarah Wentworth Apthorp Morton was another woman writer from New England, a poet compared by her admirers to Sappho and the English bluestocking Lady Mary Wortley Montagu. Sappho was not worried; neither was Lady Montagu. But in the aesthetic desert of America, any poet, of either sex, stood out like a wart on a bald head. Mrs. Morton was married to a wretched husband, a Boston merchant who had seduced and impregnated her younger sister. Gouverneur Morris paid her the compliment of sleeping with her (his lovers on both sides of the Atlantic were spirited, intelligent women). He dined with Mr. and Mrs. Morton in 1803. "Monsieur was cordial, all things considered," he noted in his diary.

A third woman writer was Phillis Wheatley, a slave. She was brought to Boston from Africa in 1761, age seven or eight. Susanna Wheatley, a merchant's wife, took pity on her, bought her, and raised her. Phillis was a precocious child; her first poems were published in 1770, blurbed by John Hancock among others. In 1775 she addressed a poem to the new American commander in chief, George Washington.

Proceed, great chief, with virtue on thy side.
Thy ev'ry action let the goddess guide.
A crown, a mansion, and a throne that shine
With gold unfading, Washington! Be thine.

Washington liked the poem, though he had some qualms about the praise. "I thank you most sincerely for your polite notice of me, in the elegant lines you enclosed; and however undeserving I may be of such encomiums and panegyricks, the style and manner exhibit a striking proof of your great poetical talents." Thomas Jefferson, on the other hand, thought Wheatley's poems were poor stuff, probably not even by her. "The compositions published under her name are below the dignity of criticism."

Warren, Morton, and Wheatley were indeed bad writers, compared to the founders at their best. But most women and men are bad writers. The founders did their best to judge American authoresses fairly, despite their sex.

Writing is a minority activity. Alexander Hamilton had a more expansive vision of women in the workforce. In his *Report on Manufactures,* he gave special attention to the rise of the factory system in Britain. One of its good consequences, he thought, was pulling the idle from the home and putting them to work. "It is worthy of particular remark, that, in general, women and children are rendered more useful . . . by manufacturing establishments than they would otherwise be. Of the number of persons employed by the cotton manufactories of Great Britain, it is computed that 4/7 nearly are women and children."

This argument strikes us, with our memories of the Triangle Shirtwaist fire a century ago and the example of Indonesian sneaker sweatshops before us today, as monstrous. In Hamilton's defense, he had seen rural squalor in the West Indies, which was no better than sweatshop squalor. His mother ran a store, and he had gone to work as a merchant's clerk at age nine. He saw no reason that other women and children shouldn't be out in the world, earning money. That was his vision of egalitarianism: all men, women, and children were created equal workers.

Congress did not share his vision, and voted no subsidies for manufacturing. The demonstration factories Hamilton planned for Paterson, New Jersey, never got off the ground, thanks to the corruption of the chief executive officer. Women would not become wage earners until the nineteenth century.

What Would the Founders Think of Children Born Out of Wedlock?

Illegitimacy was frowned upon, then as now. Several founders had good reason to know it: one was an illegitimate child, others fathered them.

Alexander Hamilton believed that his parents, a Scottish trader and a pretty Huguenot woman, had gotten married on the island of St. Kitts in the West Indies. If they did, it was illegal, since his mother's first husband, a planter living on St. Croix, had divorced her for adultery, and the laws of Denmark, which owned that island, prevented adulterers from remarrying. A cloud of gossip followed Hamilton to the mainland, and his enemies inhaled it on the many occasions when they wished to run him down. Thomas Jefferson referred, in scornful parenthesis, to Hamilton's "history, from the moment at which history can stoop to notice him." John Adams more bluntly called him "the bastard brat of a Scotch pedlar."

It was hard to be an illegitimate child, easier to create one. When Benjamin Franklin, age sixty-five, began writing his

Autobiography, he mentioned "that hard-to-be-govern'd passion of youth" that "hurried me frequently into intrigues with low women that fell in my way, which were attended with some expence and great inconvenience." Franklin's intrigues were also attended with the birth of an illegitimate son, William, when Franklin was in his early twenties. Franklin may not have needed to spell this out in his *Autobiography* because the first part of it was addressed to his son William.

John Trumbull, who painted key moments of the founding, from the signing of the Declaration to the surrender at Yorktown, had a similar experience in his twenties.

> I was a little too intimate with a girl who lived at my brother's [a servant?], and who had at the same time some other particular friends;—the natural consequence followed, and in due time a fine boy was born;—the number of fellow labourers rendered it a little difficult to ascertain precisely who was the father; but, as I was best able to pay the bill, the mother using her legal right, judiciously chose me.

Trumbull never mentioned this in his autobiography; the account comes from a letter, discovered 150 years after it was written. Both men, however little they said, took at least some responsibility for what they had done. Trumbull supported his putative son: "Having committed the folly, and acquired the name of father, I must now do the duty of one, by providing for the education of the child, to whoever he may belong." In later years, the young man, John Ray, lived with Trumbull as his nephew. Franklin acknowledged his son William and raised him; before the Revolution, when Franklin was still a loyal imperial politician, he managed to have William made royal governor of New

Jersey. Both sons repudiated their fathers politically: William Franklin was deposed by New Jersey rebels and spent the Revolution in London as a loyalist, whereas John Ray joined the British army during the War of 1812. Fatherhood is hard enough, illegitimate fatherhood more so.

As a politician, Hamilton spoke up for single mothers. In 1787 an anti-infanticide bill was debated in the New York Assembly that required the unwed mother of a dead infant to produce a witness who could testify that the child had died of natural causes. "Mr. Hamilton," wrote a newspaper, "expatiated feelingly on the delicate situation [the bill] placed an unfortunate woman in. . . . The operation of this law compelled her to publish her shame to the world." If she could be discreet instead, "she might reform and be again admitted into virtuous society." Hamilton persuaded his colleagues to strike the clause.

Two other founders represented a defendant accused of infanticide in Virginia. In 1793, Patrick Henry, still the most eloquent man in America, took the case of Richard Randolph, scion of one of the state's first families. The alleged crime was pure southern gothic, straight out of Faulkner or *Midnight in the Garden of Good and Evil*. Slaves had found the body of a white infant on a pile of shingles at a plantation. The suspected parents were Randolph's eighteen-year-old cousin, Nancy, who had been a guest at the plantation, and Randolph himself. Nancy was rumored to have given birth in the night, and the two of them had supposedly killed the newborn, or exposed it. In a display of courtroom pyrotechnics, Henry demolished the accusatory witnesses on cross-examination, while in the summation to the jury his cocounsel, young John Marshall, showed that all the evidence was hearsay or surmise (no one had saved the corpse, and the slaves who found it could not testify against white people in court). The Virginia dream team did their job well: the jury did not bother to leave the box, and acquitted Randolph.

If Richard was innocent in the eyes of the law, so also was Nancy. She was nevertheless ruined in the court of public opinion. (Years later she claimed that the baby had been stillborn, and that the father had been yet another Randolph.) She was not freed from the lingering taint of this murderous, quasi-incestuous tangle until 1809, when a third founder, Gouverneur Morris, ended his long bachelorhood by marrying her (she had moved to New York, and was working as his housekeeper). When a relative of Morris demanded to know why he had chosen such a woman for a mate, he answered, "If the world were to live with my wife, I should certainly have consulted its taste; but as that happens not to be the case, I thought I might, without offending others, endeavor to suit myself." Nancy Morris became a married mother twenty years after her scandal when she gave birth to Gouverneur Morris II in 1813.

Henry and Marshall helped an unwed mother for the usual reasons of lawyers: love of justice, combat, notoriety, and the fee. Hamilton defended unwed mothers because he honored his own. Morris married an unwed mother because he thought for himself.

What Did the Founders Think of Privacy?

In *Griswold* v. *Connecticut* (1961), Justice William O. Douglas ruled that there were "zones of privacy" created by "penumbras, formed by emanations" from the Bill of Rights. Hence, Connecticut could not prevent married couples from buying contraceptives. In later years, the courts have extended the penumbra of privacy to include abortion and gay sex. The founders had their own conception of privacy, founded on an old phrase, "the peace of families."

In the eighteenth century the phrase was used by Samuel Johnson. "He talked of the heinousness of the crime of adultery, by which the peace of families was destroyed." In 1804, it was used by Alexander Hamilton in the last significant legal case of his life. Hamilton's client was a Federalist editor who was being railroaded by the attorney general of New York for libeling President Jefferson. Hamilton began his summation by defining "the liberty of the press" as "publishing the truth, for good motives and for justifiable ends. . . . If it be not allowed," he told the court, we would lose "the privilege of canvassing [judging] our rulers." It was therefore necessary to establish whether what his client had written of Jefferson was true. (The editor had said that when Jefferson was vice president, he had paid a journalist to attack George Washington and John Adams, which was quite true.) Hamilton went on to speak for several hours; one of the judges called his speech "a master piece of pathetic, impassioned and sublime eloquence. . . . I never heard him so great."

Hamilton did not think it should be legal to publish all true statements, however. If an editor "uses the weapon of truth wantonly"—that is, "for relating that which does not appertain to official conduct," or for "disturbing the peace of families"—then this was not "fair and honest exposure," and should be judged libelous.

What truths went beyond the bounds of official conduct? What could disturb the peace of families? Publicizing love affairs, for instance. Ironically, Hamilton had done that very thing to his own family seven years earlier. In 1797 he published a ninety-five-page pamphlet, entitled *Observations on Certain Documents . . . ,* explaining how he had fallen into a honey trap laid by James and Maria Reynolds, a husband-and-wife team of blackmailers. Hamilton had laid Mrs. Reynolds, then paid $1,000 ($18,500 today) for the silence of Mr. Reynolds. (While all this was going on, Hamilton's wife, Eliza, had given birth to their fifth child.) Hamilton proclaimed this misdeed to prove that he was innocent of a worse one: his enemies had accused him of insider trading as treasury secretary, using James Reynolds as his agent. To demonstrate that his relationship with the Reynoldses was not corrupt, he had to show that it was sneaking and adulterous instead.

Hamilton was willing to sacrifice the peace of his own family in order to defend his public reputation. He did not think anyone else should be free to make such accusations. The peace of his family, though it may have been shaken (we don't know what the Hamiltons said to each other in private), was not destroyed. Eliza Hamilton stood by her man for the rest of his life, and for the fifty years she survived him.

The "peace of families" is a narrowly defined concept; "zones of privacy" are larger and more amorphous (abortion and gay sex may not have anything to do with families). Both seek to carve out territory that should be safe from intruding eyes, public or private.

CHAPTER 9

Race and Identity

Women had a role in the political community of the founders' America, though nothing like the role they have today. Who else did the founders exclude, in whole or part? Who made the grade as Americans?

In the second *Federalist* paper, John Jay wrote a striking description of the American people. "Providence has been pleased to give this one connected country to one united people—a people descended from the same ancestors, speaking the same language, professing the same religion, attached to the same principles of government, very similar in their manners and customs."

You can see why Jay wrote this. Congress conducted all its business in English; almost everyone who had any religion at all was Protestant; half of all Americans were of English stock, and another fifth came from elsewhere in the British Isles. But Jay's summary did not cover everyone. It wasn't true of the Indians who still lived in his own state. It wasn't true of his slaves. It wasn't true of John Jay, whose ancestors were French and Dutch.

The founders had fewer races, religions, and ethnicities to deal with than we do, but they too grappled with the problems of diversity and identity.

What Would the Founders Think of Reparations for Slavery?

On the day Congress declared that all men are created equal, slaves lived in all of the thirteen states. Hundreds were owned by founders—of the five-man drafting committee that produced the Declaration, John Adams and Roger Sherman had never been slave owners; Benjamin Franklin was a former slave owner; Thomas Jefferson and Robert Livingston owned dozens apiece. Yet most of the founders thought slavery was wrong: it brought "the judgment of heaven on a country," as George Mason, a slave owner, put it. Living in the midst of the institution, their thoughts on how it might end, and whether slaves could be compensated somehow, were vague, fearful, and occasionally practical.

In their idealistic moments the founders hoped the spirit of the Revolution itself might end slavery, by a contagion of liberty; "I think a change [is] already perceptible," wrote Jefferson in 1784. By the end of the decade, three states had abolished slavery, and Congress had forbidden it in the northwest territories (now Ohio, Indiana, Illinois, Michigan, and Wisconsin). Yet abolition never crossed the Mason-Dixon line or the Ohio River. In 1818, when Missouri applied to become the first new state entirely west of the Mississippi, two signers of the Constitution still sat in Congress, and joined in the bitter debate over whether Missouri should be admitted with slaves or without. Charles Pinckney of South Carolina voted for slavery; Rufus King of New York voted against. The spirit of the revolution, it seemed, meant different things to different revolutionaries.

Some founders feared that slaves would take reparations, or at least vengeance, through bloodshed. Slave revolts were the nightmare of every slave society (James Monroe had to suppress one when he was governor of Virginia); the founders had ring-side seats for a spectacularly violent, and successful, revolt in Saint Domingue (Haiti) that began in the 1790s. The island's blacks and mulattoes, after a decade of fighting French, British, Spaniards, and each other, expelled or killed the white planter class. Many Americans, not only slave owners, dreaded the same thing happening in America. John Adams, in an 1821 letter to his old friend Jefferson, sidled from a humorous discussion of religious visionaries into a weird prophecy of his own. "Slavery in this country I have seen hanging over it like a black cloud for half a century. If I were as drunk with enthusiasm as [John Wesley] I might probably say I had seen armies of Negroes marching and countermarching in the air, shining in armor."

Jefferson had anticipated his friend's vision, and the Haitian revolution, with his own forebodings in *Notes on Virginia*. "Can the liberties of a nation be thought secure," he asked,

> when we have removed their only firm basis, a conviction in the minds of the people that these liberties are of the gift of God? That they are not to be violated but with His wrath? Indeed I tremble for my country when I reflect that God is just; that his justice cannot sleep forever; that considering numbers, nature and natural means only, a revolution of the wheel of fortune, an exchange of situation is among possible events; that it

may become probable by supernatural interference! The Almighty has no attribute which can take sides with us in such a contest.

Jefferson's passion may be gauged by his prose: he never summons the Almighty or exclamation points casually. His reasoning is borrowed from John Locke, who had written that revolts against injustice were just. "Shaking off a power, which force, and not right hath set over any one, though it hath the name of *Rebellion*, yet is no offence before God, but is that which he allows and countenances." But Jefferson writes with more emotion than Locke—naturally enough, since he is among those who might be shaken off.

The only compensation the founders contemplated for the decades of unpaid labor from which so many Americans had profited was education. George Washington's will directed that the young slaves he was freeing be taught to read and write, and "be brought up to some useful occupation." A few antislavery founders went beyond providing for their own property. In 1785, thirty-two New Yorkers, including John Jay, Alexander Hamilton, and Governor George Clinton, founded the New-York Manumission Society. (Jay and Clinton both owned slaves, but they did not feel hypocritical to be founding a manumission society on that account; their goal was to end an institution, not to purge themselves.) One of the New-York Manumission Society's first projects was an African Free School that taught free black boys and girls to read, write, and shun "habits of idleness." By 1823, the school had almost nine hundred pupils, more than half the black children of school age in New York City. Its graduates included professionals, clergymen, and one of the founders of

Liberia, as well as ordinary workers; in the 1840s it was folded into the public school system.

The founders did not successfully deal with slavery, and only marginally with its effects.

Would the Founders Allow Indians to Build Casinos?

Indian casinos, operating in states that do not allow gambling, are a sign of the special legal status of Indian tribes.

Of all the founders George Washington had the most experience dealing with Indians. They were allies and enemies in the French and Indian War and the Revolution; as president, he sent armies against them and signed treaties with them. John Quincy Adams, John Adams's eldest son, attended a reception for five Chickasaw chiefs in 1794, at which President Washington and his guests smoked a peace pipe. "Whether this ceremony be really of Indian origin," wrote young Adams, "I confess I have some doubt. At least these Indians appeared to be quite unused to it, and from their manner of going through it, looked as if they were submitting to a process in compliance with *our* custom."

When Washington was a young man, he chafed at British restrictions on colonists buying Indian land. When he was older, and America had become independent, he favored regulating the process, seeing frontiersmen as "banditti" whose greed for land would involve the government in needless conflict. "Policy and economy [both] point very strongly to the expediency of being upon good terms with the Indians, and the propriety of purchasing their lands," rather than driving them off. In the end, however, Washington believed the Indians would be driven off, slowly rather than suddenly, for agriculture was the enemy of hunter-gatherers, making their game scarce and making them move on. "The gradual extension of our settlements will as certainly cause the savage as the wolf to retire; both being beasts of prey tho' they differ in shape."

Thomas Jefferson looked at Indians as a scientist, not a soldier; he was curious about their languages and customs, and admired, even sentimentalized, their virtues. "[They have] never submitted themselves to any laws, any coercive power, any shadow of government. Their only controls are their manners, and that moral sense of right and wrong, which, like the sense of tasting and feeling in every man, makes a part of his nature." But he shared Washington's view of their destiny on a continent increasingly inhabited by white men. "Our settlements," he wrote, "will gradually circumscribe and approach the Indians and they will in time either incorporate with us as citizens of the Untied States or remove beyond the Mississippi. The former is certainly the termination of their history most happy for themselves." Neither Washington nor Jefferson wanted to pick fights with Indians, but they expected them to assimilate, or to recede. Since Americans were bound to follow them across the Mississippi, all the way to the Pacific, they would ultimately recede from the map of American history.

Among the Indian leaders who saw this fate looming, and who tried to avert it, was the Mohawk Joseph Brant, who advocated an alliance of Indians with the British during the Revolutionary War. The policy failed then, but it was revived on the eve of the War of 1812 by Tecumseh, a Shawnee, who tried to rally all the Indians of the frontier, from the Great Lakes to Alabama, into a united confederacy. In 1813, the Americans killed him at the Battle of the Thames in Ontario, east of Detroit. As the war wound down, Tecumseh's British allies, negotiating the peace treaty with the Americans in the Belgian city of Ghent, demanded an independent Indian nation in what is now the Midwest. This show of concern brought a snort from Gouverneur Morris when he learned of it. "The British ministers have, it seems, discovered, in the commencement of the nineteenth century, that our copper-coloured brothers are human beings." They had had two centuries to notice; what took them so long? Who knew what they, and we, might notice next? "Take care, my good friend, that they do not make a similar discovery respecting our ebony-coloured brethren." The British dropped their demand, and the last hope for real Indian independence in North America vanished.

But there was another option. Suppose Indians, without becoming American citizens, stopped living as hunter-gatherers or, as Washington put it, "beasts of prey"? Suppose they added, to what Jefferson called their manners and moral sense, laws and government? The Cherokees of northwest Georgia took this path, adopting all the habits of their white neighbors: they farmed, owned slaves, wrote a constitution, and published a newspaper (the editor had taken the name Elias Boudinot, after a founding congressman he had met through Christian missionary work). In 1828 gold was discovered on Cherokee land, which the State of Georgia coveted; the Cherokees appealed to the courts. In a pair of decisions written in 1831–1832, Chief Justice John Marshall lamented the spectacle of "a people once numerous, powerful and truly independent," fighting for "a remnant" of their former status, and ruled that the Cherokees were a "distinct political community" under the authority of the federal government; therefore, Georgia could not eject them. But President Andrew Jackson found Cherokees, including Boudinot, who were willing to sign a treaty of self-eviction. The tribe was forcibly moved, with great loss of life, to what is now Oklahoma, where the signers of the treaty were assassinated.

Marshall's view of Indians as "distinct political communit[ies]" lost out in his day, but flourishes at Foxwoods now.

What Would the Founders Think of the Bell Curve?

The founders thought the opening paragraphs of the Declaration of Independence were a parade of self-evident truths. Congress cut-and-pasted the indictment of George III, which is the meat of the document, and the conclusion, but it left Jefferson's thoughts on rights and equality intact, because all the founders were equally convinced of them. "All men are born equally free and independent," wrote John Adams when he was drafting the Massachusetts Constitution of 1779. "The benevolent creator and father of men ha[s] given to them all an equal right to life, liberty and property," declared the New-York Manumission Society in 1785. These were statements of rights, not abilities. The founders were not saying that all men were equally talented or intelligent, nor did they care: as Jefferson put it, talents were "no measure" of human rights. "Because Sir Isaac Newton was superior to others in understanding, he was not therefore lord of the person or property of others." But what did the founders—who were all white—think of the abilities of men who belonged to other races?

By the time of the Revolution, Americans had been dealing with Indians and Africans for more than 150 years. They saw them variously as enemies to be feared, brutes to be scorned, children to be trained, natural men to be admired, or slaves to be worked; Caliban, the indigenous character in Shakespeare's *Tem-*

pest (based on a shipwreck in Bermuda), is all five. Missionaries also saw them as souls to be saved.

The Revolution was a practical test of their ability as soldiers. When George Washington came north in the spring of 1775 to take command of the troops besieging Boston, he was surprised to find black soldiers in the ranks. "We have some Negroes," wrote General John Thomas, commander of a Massachusetts unit, "but I look upon them in general [as] equally serviceable with other men. . . . [M]any of them have proved themselves brave." Washington ordered no more blacks to be enlisted, but chronic shortfalls of manpower soon changed his mind. Of the twelve thousand men he commanded at the Battle of Monmouth (June 1778), eight hundred were blacks or Indians (a few of their names: Cash Affrica, Shadrack Battle, Oliver Cromwell, Artillo Freeman). The black soldiers were mostly freemen; some were slaves fighting in their masters' places. Washington was the last American to command integrated units until the Korean War.

Washington also planned to assemble a light infantry corps, for skirmishing, with a unit of four hundred Indians attached. "Such a body of Indians, joined by some of our woodsmen [frontier riflemen] would probably strike no small terror into the British and foreign troops." The Indians were to be commanded by Captain Abraham Nimham, a Mohican chief's son, but he and his followers were ambushed and killed by the enemy in August 1778 before the project could take shape.

In 1779 two young colonels on Washington's staff proposed a more radical idea—to raise as many as four battalions of black slaves in South Carolina, who would be given "their freedom with their muskets." John Laurens volunteered to command the unit; his friend Alexander Hamilton talked it up. Both men knew slavery from the inside; Laurens's father, Henry, was one of the largest slave traders in South Carolina; Hamilton had grown up on Nevis and St. Croix, two Caribbean sugar islands. Hamilton lobbied Congressman John Jay for the project. "I frequently hear it objected to the scheme of [enlisting] negroes," Hamilton wrote, "that they are too stupid to make soldiers." If that were true, he went on breezily, that would be no problem, since no less an authority than Frederick the Great had said that stupid soldiers could fight well. But Hamilton did not think it was true. "Their natural faculties are probably as good as ours. . . . The contempt we have been taught to entertain for the blacks, makes us fancy many things that are founded neither in reason nor experience; and an unwillingness to part with property of so valuable a kind will furnish a thousand arguments" against parting with it. In three sentences, Hamilton explains the economic origins of racism: blacks are as smart as anyone; the belief that they are not is a prejudice; the prejudice is founded on self-interest.

The two colonels persuaded Washington to endorse their scheme, but the legislature of South Carolina would not consent. "I was outvoted," Laurens wrote Hamilton, "having only reason on my side."

Washington's body servant throughout the war was Billy Lee, a mulatto he had bought when Lee was a teenager in 1768. Lee was an excellent horseman, like his master, and was at Washington's side during his battles. The *Recollections* of George W. P. Custis, Washington's step-grandson, contains a sentimental vignette of Lee as an old man, crippled and alcoholic, but still anxious to reminisce with every veteran who visited Mount Vernon. "The new-time people don't know what we old soldiers did and suffered for the country in the old war. Was it not cold enough at Valley Forge? Yes, was it; and I am sure you remember it was hot enough at Monmouth [the Battle of Monmouth had been fought in one hundred–degree heat]." "My mulatto man William" is the second beneficiary mentioned in Washington's will, after his wife, Martha. Lee was offered a choice of immediate freedom or a lifelong berth at Mount Vernon, with a thirty-dollar annuity in either case. "This I give him," Washington concluded, "for his faithful services during the Revolutionary War." Lee had served him faithfully before and after the war; Washington specifically identified him as a veteran.

In some states, blacks were thought competent to exercise peacetime public responsibilities: they were allowed to vote. In 1800, Robert Livingston sent his "elegant chariot" to take an elderly black man in New York City to the polls. This was part of a high-power populist campaign the Republican Party waged that year to put Thomas Jefferson in the White House. The old man disappointed Livingston by voting Federalist, as most New York blacks did, in recognition of the leading role Jay and other Federalists had played in passing the state's abolition law the year before. Free black New Yorkers kept the right to vote for another twenty years, until Jefferson's political heirs in the state finally wrested it from them.

Fighting and voting were concrete instances of presumed equality of ability. Jefferson tried to examine the question of black ability scientifically in *Notes of Virginia*, and produced a long discussion that has dogged his reputation from his lifetime until now. Jefferson begins by exploring "real distinctions which nature has made" between blacks and whites, both mental and physical. Only one of these is to the credit of blacks: "In music they are more generally gifted than the white." Since Jefferson was a passionate musician himself, this is a real concession. He makes no others. Some of his judgments are fantastic: blacks cannot speak well; they have "no poetry." Some are cringe making:

blacks prefer white women as lovers, even as orangutans prefer black women. Some show an embarrassing lack of awareness: black skin "covers the emotions." Perhaps Jefferson's slaves did not wish to show him all their emotions; perhaps he did not wish to understand the emotions they showed.

After this creepy catalog, Jefferson changes course. He has been talking about the physical traits, and the "endowments of the head" of black people; where endowments "of the heart" were concerned, nature has "done them justice." Masters complain that slaves steal, but that is a by-product of slavery. "The man in whose favor no laws of property exist, probably feels himself less bound to respect those made in favor of others." Even so, "we find among them numerous instances of the most rigid integrity, and as many as among their better instructed masters, of benevolence, gratitude, and unshaken fidelity." It is a long time in coming, but Jefferson decides that, in the traits that he told Maria Cosway were most important, blacks are his equals.

Nevertheless, Jefferson ends with a grim judgment: because of physical and mental differences, as well as the malign legacies of history (white prejudice, black resentment), blacks should be freed—and sent somewhere else. Lafayette thought of establishing a settlement for freed blacks in Guiana; in the early nineteenth century, liberated American and British slaves were sent to Liberia and Sierra Leone. Colonization, as it was called, rejected the possibility of assimilation, and put a prohibitive cost on manumission. At the end of his life, Jefferson was too broke to have freed all his slaves, even if he had wanted to. Virginia would never be rich enough to buy out all slave owners and send the freemen back to Africa.

One founder tried to make a person of color his heir. George Wythe trained Jefferson in the law, signed the Declaration of

Independence, and attended the Constitutional Convention. He died in 1806, leaving a will that gave half his bank stock to Michael Brown, a young mulatto servant whom Wythe had freed years earlier. Wythe's will also asked Jefferson to take charge of Brown's education. Brown did not inherit, however, because he and Wythe died at the same time—poisoned by arsenic. The murderer was George Sweeney, Wythe's grandnephew, who stood to inherit the rest of Wythe's bank stock. The cook, Lydia Broadnax, another freed black servant, had seen Sweeney pour a powder in the breakfast coffee, but under Virginia law no black person could testify against a white person in court. Sweeney walked.

No child of Wythe's two marriages had survived infancy. It is hard to escape the conclusion that Brown was Wythe's son, whom he wished to leave in the charge of no one less than the president of the United States. Wythe's white heir prevented it, and the Virginia legal system let the white heir go free. The founding did not live up to this particular founder.

What Kind of Immigration Policy Would the Founders Have Had?

The founders accepted the old ethnic communities in their midst—Dutch in New York, Germans in Pennsylvania. Several of the founders belonged to them: the First Congress contained two Muhlenbergs, a Schuyler, and a Van Rensselaer.

Founders welcomed new immigrants that met their business needs. In 1784 George Washington was in the market for a carpenter and a bricklayer. He asked Tench Tilghman, one of his wartime aides, to scour a boatload of Germans that was due to land in Baltimore for the proper workmen. "I would not confine you to" Germans, he added. "If they are good workmen, they may be of Asia, Africa, or Europe. They may be Mahometans, Jews, or Christian of any sect—or they may be atheists." Washington was laying it on for comic effect; he is saying, hire *anybody* who can put boards or bricks together. But there is no reason to think that if Tilghman had found a Muslim bricklayer, Washington wouldn't have hired him.

New arrivals always raised the question of assimilation, however. A proxy discussion of assimilation occurred at the Constitutional Convention when Gouverneur Morris moved to raise the citizenship requirement for senators from four years to fourteen. George Mason supported the motion, even toying with the idea of restricting the Senate to the native born. Benjamin Franklin opposed the motion, calling immigration "a proof of attachment" to America that "ought to excite our confidence and affection." (Early in his career, Franklin had scoffed at Pennsylvania Germans as "boors" and had lost an election to the colonial assembly because of it; he seemed to have learned his lesson.)

Two immigrants spoke to Morris's motion. Pierce Butler, who had come from Ireland, wanted a long residence requirement for senators. Foreigners "bring with them, not only attachments to other countries, but ideas of government so distinct from ours that in every point of view they are dangerous." James Wilson, who had come from Scotland, defended the sensibilities of immigrants. "To be appointed to a place may be [a] matter of indifference. To be incapable of being appointed is a circumstance grating and mortifying." Morris defended his motion in high style.

We should not be polite at the expense of prudence. . . . It is said that some tribes of Indians carried their hospitality so far as to offer to strangers their wives and daughters. Was this a proper model for us? He would admit them to his house, he would invite them to his table, would provide for them comfortable lodgings, but would not carry the complaisance so far as to bed them with his wife.

The Constitution fixed the citizenship requirement for representatives at seven years, and for senators at nine. The president had to be a native, or "a citizen of the United States, at the time of the adoption of this Constitution" (so James Wilson would be spared the mortification of not being eligible). Congress was given the power to establish a "uniform Rule of Naturalization."

Fear of foreigners increased after the French Revolution. French diplomats meddled in American politics, attacking President Washington, and taking sides in the election of 1796; perhaps ordinary Frenchmen, caught up in the ferment of their native land, or Irishmen, fleeing their own political troubles, might do the same. Harrison Gray Otis, a Massachusetts Federalist, said he did "not wish to invite hordes of wild Irishmen, nor the turbulent and disorderly of all parts of the world, to come here with a view to disturb our tranquility." Federalists mocked Representative Albert Gallatin's thick French accent, the heritage of his birth in Geneva (Abigail Adams called him "the Swiss incendiary"). The Naturalization Act of 1798 raised the residency requirement for citizenship from five years to fourteen. After the Louisiana Purchase, Fisher Ames wrote that "the otters would as soon obey" our laws as the French and Spanish "savages and adventurers" who lived there.

The Republicans profited from Federalist alarm by courting the ethnic vote. In the same New York election in which Robert Livingston sent his carriage for an old black voter, Aaron Burr sent German-speaking orators to the city's Seventh Ward, the German neighborhood. Burr's maneuver worked better than Livingston's. The ethnic vote helped boost the Republicans to power in New York and Pennsylvania, and ultimately nationwide. Thomas Jefferson understood Gallatin well enough to make him his treasury secretary.

The eternal themes of immigration politics—anxiety over assimilation, and flattery of immigrants—were set by the founders.

Would the Founders Favor the English-Only Movement?

When John Jay wrote, in Federalist no. 2, that Americans spoke "the same language," he was false to the moment at which he wrote—fall 1787—and to any subsequent moment of American history. Foreign languages were spoken in the earshot of the founders, and have been spoken here ever since. But Jay was true to the history of his family.

Jay's maternal grandfather, Jacobus van Cortlandt, was born in New York when it was still Nieuw Amsterdam, a Dutch colony. England took the town when Van Cortlandt was two years old, and forty years later he ran for a seat in the colonial assembly. The English governor of the colony scoffed that he could "scarce speak English." Ninety years later, his grandson helped write, in English, a book that is in every bookstore, and on the curriculum of every college.

The founders learned foreign languages to stretch their minds: John Adams and Thomas Jefferson corresponded about the classics; Gouverneur Morris wrote little poems in French and German for his cosmopolitan friends. They used foreign languages when it suited their political or commercial interests: Benjamin Franklin, for all his Germanophobia, published the

Philadelphische Zeitung, America's first German-language news-paper, because he hoped it would make money (it failed). They spoke it among themselves when it made some point: at the Constitutional Convention Franklin told a joke with a French punch line because it turned on the self-esteem of a vain woman, and what woman is vainer (or has more reason to be) than a Frenchwoman? But they conducted their political business, which was their most important business, in English; they bid for immortality in their mother tongue.

Most of the founders were good writers; a few of them were great. They could keep a straight face. "In the first place, gentle-men, you are to consider that a great empire, like a great cake, is most easily diminished at the edges. Turn your attention there-fore first to your remotest provinces; that as you get rid of them, the next may follow in order." They could make men willing to die. "What is it that the gentlemen wish? What would they have? Is life so dear or peace so sweet as to be purchased at the price of chains and slavery?" "The summer soldier and sunshine patriot will, in this crisis, shrink from the service of their country; but he that stands it now, deserves the love and thanks of man and woman." They could tell men what to live for. "The God who gave us life gave us liberty at the same time; the hand of force may destroy, but cannot disjoin them." "To secure the blessings of liberty to ourselves and our posterity." A common quality in all their best writing is captured by the word *nervous,* which in the eighteenth century meant "vigorous, energetic." But we should not ignore its modern sense of "high-strung, excitable." They were energetic because they were working for a great cause; they were high-strung because they had no real models, and they did not know whether they could succeed. Everything was a first draft that had to be rushed to print, or posted online.

If America becomes a truly bi- or multilingual society, all Americans (not just a handful of well-educated rich ones, like Adams and Jefferson construing Greek or Morris dashing off French love poems) will have to learn English if they wish to touch the founders' minds.

CHAPTER 10

Politics

So we come to what occupied these driven, eloquent men, in office or out, thinking, writing or doing, at work or at leisure: politics.

But how can the founders be politicians? Politicians are the town supervisor, the city councilman, the surrogate court judge, the state legislator, Bush or Kerry (pick one, or both), the perennial office seeker and the perennial officeholder. Politicians are friends to everyone, loyal only to themselves. A politician is an arse upon / which everyone has sat except a man (e. e. cummings). Politicians are like crabgrass, unsightly, unkillable, ubiquitous.

The founders weren't that. They were patriots, statesmen, leaders. They had marble heads and bronze fingers. They gaze down at us from heaven or Mount Rushmore, and we rub their faces in our pockets.

Some of the founders were ascending to this condition while they lived. William Pierce, a delegate to the Constitutional Convention, wrote this description of his fellow delegate Benjamin Franklin:

> Dr. Franklin is well known to be the greatest philosopher of the present age—all the operations of nature he seems to understand—the very heavens obey him, and the clouds yield up their lightning to be imprisoned in his rod. But what claim he has to the politician, posterity must determine. It is certain that he does not shine much in council—he is no speaker, nor does he seem to let politics engage his attention.

If Franklin had read this, he would have enjoyed it immensely, for it conceals everything and tells nothing—just what Franklin the politician would have wished. Indeed, he might have written it himself, had not Pierce so obligingly (and so innocently) done it for him.

The founders wanted greatness for America and immortality for themselves, but politics was the way they got it, and they were (intermittently) honest enough to know it.

What Would the Founders Think about Partisanship?

Sick of attack ads, spinning, mindless partisanship? The founders hated it as much as you do. They also invented it.

It was with them almost from the start, in George Washington's first term as president, in the heart of his inner circle, and it alarmed him. In 1792 his treasury secretary, Alexander Hamilton, and his secretary of state, Thomas Jefferson, began abusing each other in the newspapers. The quarrel started with fiscal policy, but soon branched out to character assassination. (Hamilton wrote his own op-eds; Jefferson got friends, like Representative James Madison, to write for him.) The Jeffersonians thought that Hamilton might undermine the infant republic; Hamilton thought the same of Jefferson. All the writers used pseudonyms, but everyone quickly figured out who was saying what. Things got so hot that, in midsummer, Washington asked both men what was going on, heard what they had to say, then begged them to cool off. He wanted, he wrote in identical phrases to Hamilton and Jefferson, "mutual forbearances and temporizing yieldings *on all sides.*"

He didn't get them. The contestants fell briefly silent, then, in Washington's second term, went back at it even more boisterously than before. The public got involved; there were riots over foreign policy, and an armed uprising over taxes. Washington returned to the topic of partisanship in 1796, in his Farewell Address, in which he decried "the baneful effects of the spirit of party." It "distract[s] the public councils and enfeeble[s] the public administration." It breeds "ill founded jealousies and false alarms." It "kindles the animosity" of different sections of the country against each other. It "foments occasionally riot and insurrection" (all he had to do was think of the last four years). "[I]t is a spirit," he concluded, solemnly and lamely, "not to be encouraged." He was solemn, because he thought partisanship was truly dangerous; he was lame, because he rather suspected that it wasn't going away anytime soon.

All the founders disliked parties as much as Washington did. "If I could not go to heaven but with a party," wrote Jefferson, "I would not go there at all." John Adams said he would "quarrel with both parties and with every individual of each" before enlisting in either. At most, they admitted that partisan activity might be an emergency measure, necessary to throw a set of rascals out. But once the rascals were gone, parties should go with them. After Jefferson won the White House in an election (1800) even more vicious and scary than the election of 2000, he assured the nation in his inaugural address, referring to the two parties that had almost torn it apart, "we are all republicans—we are all federalists." Privately he wrote that he would "sink federalism into an abyss from which there shall be no resurrection for it." Jefferson seemed to have succeeded in his nonpartisan dream: his second successful presidential campaign (1804) and Madison's first (1808) were easy victory laps; their rival (Charles Cotesworth Pinckney was the Federalist candidate against both men) carried no more than a handful of states. But by the time Madison stood for reelection in 1812, partisanship was back. He squeaked in on the strength of one state (Pennsylvania), and his second term was enlivened by calls for secession.

Partisanship is collective action in the service of political victory—defining friends and enemies, and keeping the former out of power with the help of the latter. It exists in all political bodies, and under all political systems, from town meetings to politburos to the Vatican. Stable partisanship arises when the contestants also learn to accept defeat—to go home gracefully and to assume that the winners, though they may be fools or bums, are not criminals and traitors. It didn't take much time for the founders to learn how to win; it took longer to learn how to lose.

Hamilton took a first step in the election of 1800. He faced a bad choice. Jefferson, his enemy for almost a decade, was the candidate of the Republican Party; President Adams, running for reelection as the candidate of the Federalists, seemed to him to have gone off the rails. Hamilton played very hard ball in this campaign. When the Republicans won control of the New York legislature (which would pick the state's presidential electors) he wrote John Jay, the governor, urging him to change the election laws after the fact to allow for a popular vote in electoral districts, some of which he expected the Federalists to carry. (This is the letter in which he called Jefferson an "atheist" and a "fanatic" [see "Should Religion be in Politics?" above].) He also hoped to manipulate the votes of Federalist presidential electors so that Adams's running mate would win more votes than Adams. Both these schemes failed (Jay's dry comment on Hamilton's New York plan was that it "would not become me to adopt" it).

The vote in the electoral college presented Hamilton a new bad choice. The founders had by this time invented partisan presidential tickets, with a party nominee and a running mate, though the Constitution did not formally recognize them. Before the Twelfth Amendment (1802), every elector cast two votes, just as every elector does today. But the presidency went to the man who won the most electoral votes, while the second-place finisher became vice president. In 1800, however, every Republican elector voted for their party's number-one and number-two choices, producing a tie between their leader, Jefferson, and his running mate, Aaron Burr. The tie had to be broken in the House of Representatives, where Republicans and Federalists were evenly balanced—and Federalists began toying with the notion of picking the relatively unknown quantity, Burr, over the hated Jefferson. Hamilton swallowed hard—and urged his party to let Jefferson win. He was, he admitted, no fan of the man: he still thought Jefferson was "mischievous," "crafty," "not scrupulous," not "very mindful of truth," and "a contemptible hypocrite." But, he argued, Jefferson was no "zealot. . . . He is as likely as any man I know to temporize." (Hamilton forgot that he had called him a "fanatic" a few months earlier.) There was also "no fair reason to suppose" that Jefferson was "capable of being corrupted."

Hamilton was taking a first step in the direction of the modern election-night ritual, the concession speech. Jefferson was wrong, but he wasn't wicked; let him win. Hamilton's step didn't take him or the country very far. He was equally motivated by the belief that Aaron Burr was very wicked indeed (a case of "great ambition unchecked by principle"). The Federalists in the House surrendered in the most graceless way possible, abstaining rather than voting for the winner. John Adams, the outgoing president, left town rather than attend his successor's inauguration.

On the other hand, there had been no hanky-panky, no coups. Everyone had followed (barely) the rules. The founders still had a lot to learn about partisanship, but they had begun.

What Did the Founders Think of the Politics of Personal Destruction?

In his first inaugural address (1801), Thomas Jefferson expressed a poignant hope: in the aftermath of what had been the most acrid presidential election in the nation's history, Jefferson asked his fellow Americans to "restore to social intercourse that harmony and affection without which liberty and even life itself are but dreary things." It wouldn't be so easy, as he would soon learn.

Some of the founders were among the best writers and talkers America has ever produced, and when they reamed each other in private, they did it good and hard. When they wanted to do so in public, they turned to contemptible men of no social standing, that is, journalists.

The most effective, and the most contemptible, hit man was James Callender. Callender was a Scottish pamphleteer who left

Britain in the 1790s after insulting George III. He came to America, where he enlisted his pen on the side of Jefferson, who slipped him small sums of money. The first significant target of his insults here was Alexander Hamilton, whom he accused in a pamphlet of insider trading, with the help of a common crook, James Reynolds (Hamilton, as treasury secretary, supposedly gave Reynolds timely tips, and Reynolds went out and made the trades). But Callender had gotten his facts wrong. As Hamilton revealed in his counterpamphlet, Reynolds actually slipped Hamilton Maria Reynolds, his wife, and Hamilton gave Reynolds money—rather a lot, one thousand dollars, one-third of his salary—for Reynolds's acquiescence, and his silence. "The charge against me," Hamilton wrote, "is . . . improper pecuniary speculation. My real crime is an amorous connection with [Reynolds's] wife."

The confession that Callender had extorted delighted Hamilton's enemies: it was a "curious specimen of the ingenious folly of its author," James Madison wrote Jefferson. But Callender was not done with the founders. After the election of 1800, he told Madison, now secretary of state, that he would like to be rewarded with a postmaster's job. The job did not come through; perhaps the Jeffersonians realized what kind of man they had been dealing with; in any case, they no longer needed him. Miffed, Callender looked around for anti-Jefferson gossip and took his revenge two years later, when he told the nation about Sally Hemings. "It is well known that the man, whom it de-lighteth the people to honor, keeps and for many years has kept, as his concubine, one of his slaves. Her name is SALLY. The name of her eldest son is Tom. His features are said to bear a striking though sable resemblance to those of the president himself." Federalist editors gleefully reprinted Callender's story, with a running commentary of rollicking, racist songs. More painful to Jefferson must have been the rebuke he received from his now estranged friend, Abigail Adams: "The serpent you cherished and warmed, bit the hand that nourished him."

The politics of personal destruction don't always destroy, as Bill Clinton demonstrated. Jefferson won the election of 1804 by a crushing margin, no matter what Callender had said about him, because he had cut taxes and the country was at peace. Nor was Hamilton destroyed by his sex scandal. Some historians say that the Reynolds affair prevented Hamilton from ever seeking high elective office, but he never had sought it. He flourished as an administrator, a polemicist, or a wire-puller, not as a leading man. Hamilton pursued his preferred roles until the day he died.

That day came when it did because of another form of the politics of personal destruction, unknown to us but common among the founders: dueling. Benjamin Franklin described the practice with a story about two men in a coffeehouse. One asks the other to sit farther away, because he smells. "That, Sir," says the second man, "is an affront, and you must fight me." The first man agrees, but doesn't think fighting will help—"for if you kill me, I shall smell too; and if I kill you, you will smell, if possible, more than you do at present." Like all great comics, Franklin mocks an ideal by breaking it down to its physical traits: duels kill, and death stinks. But to those who believed in dueling, it was a way of upholding honor: the last resort of the offended.

The Revolution gave dueling a big push in American life, since officers care passionately about honor, and they're used to firearms. George Washington never dueled, but many of his officers did, some of them on behalf of Washington's honor, challenging other officers who had criticized his conduct too sharply. In peacetime, or away from the battlefield, dueling became a fea-

ture of political warfare. Leaders considered themselves gentlemen; leadership could be undermined or secured by besmirching
or defending a leader's honor. As a consequence, charges and
countercharges flowed torrentially. Some accusations—anything
written by a journalist—were considered beneath notice (Hamilton's retort to Callender was exceptional). But if a fellow politician—that is, a fellow gentleman—went too far, he had to be
challenged. The requirements of honor were so strict that even
though dueling was everywhere illegal it was widely practiced.

Some duels strike us as almost comic. DeWitt Clinton and
John Swartout were not founders, but they were junior partners
of founders, DeWitt Clinton the right-hand man of his uncle
George Clinton, and Swartout an ally of Aaron Burr. In 1802 the
younger Clinton and Swartout went to Weehawken, New Jersey,
a popular spot for New York City duelists (it had a remote ledge
some yards up from the Hudson River where they were unlikely
to be disturbed). The first three times Clinton and Swartout
fired, no one was hurt. On the fourth exchange, Swartout was
shot in the leg, but he insisted on continuing. On the fifth exchange, Swartout was hit in the leg again, but he wanted to keep
going. Clinton left the field in disgust. We might think of the
torso knight in *Monty Python and the Holy Grail*, but Swartout's
allies were not amused: they blasted Clinton for his ungentle-
manly withdrawal.

Duelists did not suffer for their lawbreaking. In 1798 Brock-
holst Livingston of the powerful New York Republican clan in-
sulted a Federalist, James Jones, who then caned him and pulled
his nose. Livingston challenged Jones to a duel. They went to
Weehawken, where Jones was killed. Eight years later Jefferson
put Livingston on the Supreme Court. Confirmation hearings
were not what they are now.

One signer of the Declaration and two signers of the Constitution died in duels. The rarest signature of any signer of the Declaration is that of Button Gwinnett, of Georgia. One reason it is so hard to find is that in 1777 Gwinnett was killed by Lachlan McIntosh, a political rival. In 1802, Richard Spaight, a signer of the Constitution from North Carolina, died in a duel with one of his rivals, John Stanly.

The most famous rivalry and the most famous duel pitted Alexander Hamilton against Aaron Burr (see "What Would the Founders Think of Gun Control?" in chapter 3). They had opposed each other in the presidential election of 1800 and the New York governor's race of 1804. Finally, Burr thought that Hamilton had made statements that reflected on his honor. The two gentlemen went to Weehawken, where Hamilton was mortally wounded.

Gouverneur Morris, who had known Hamilton for almost thirty years, considered the morality of dueling and duelists the night before he delivered his friend's eulogy. Burr, he wrote in his diary, "ought to be considered in the same light with any other man who had killed another in a duel. . . . I certainly should not excite to any outrage on him," but "prudence would, I should suppose, direct him to keep out of the way." This was the world's view of dueling. It was like smoking dope—illegal, but common, so it had to be done discreetly. But Morris encountered another view when he discussed the matter with Matthew Clarkson, a New York businessman who was also a friend of the dead man. "If we were truly brave," Clarkson told Morris, "we should not accept a challenge; but we are all cowards." Clarkson had fought at Saratoga and Yorktown, but it was easier to face the enemy than defy social convention. "The tears rolling down his face,"

Morris wrote, "gave strong effect to the voice and manner with which he pronounced this sentence."

Today the politics of personal destruction is all about politics and personality, but to the founders it could lead to actual destruction. Their political conventions were even more ferocious than ours.

Would the Founders Enact Campaign-Finance Reform?

Campaigning was simple in the founding era. You treated voters to drinks on election day (illegal, but expected; young James Madison failed to do so in his first run for office, and he lost). You bought newspapers and the journalists who wrote for them, which was cheap enough. In the election of 1800 Aaron Burr organized speakers and door-to-door campaigners in New York City; he even found German speakers to go to German ethnic neighborhoods. Burr's techniques were so unusual that they were thought of as some strange black art. But even in those innocent days the political power of the rich was a topic of discussion.

At the Constitutional Convention Gouverneur Morris discussed the matter with his usual bluntness. The rich, he warned, were dangerous, and they would be made more dangerous by enfranchising the poor. "Give the votes to people who have no property, and they will sell them to the rich who will be able to buy them. . . . We should remember that the people never act from reason alone. The rich will take advantage of their passions and make these the instruments of oppressing them." Morris knew what he was talking about, for he came from a rich New York family that had been doing just that since colonial times. At the dawn of the Revolution, he had spoken of his fellow New

Yorkers as reptiles and sheep; they were both dangerous, and easily led. Morris had a low opinion of the common man, and an equally low opinion of his peers who manipulated them.

Similar concerns motivate campaign-finance reformers today: every television owner is an idiot, and every campaign manager is an evil genius. Therefore, spending must be controlled by the wise and good.

It's a wonder that James Madison—and Gouverneur Morris—ever got elected to anything.

Did the Founders Believe in Term Limits?

The eighteenth-century word for term limits was *rotation*—rotating men through the offices they held. In April 1775, in the tense days before the Battles of Lexington and Concord, when Fairfax County, Virginia, established an independent militia, rotation of officers was an issue in their deliberations, and two founders played key roles—George Mason and Colonel George Washington.

Any tenure of office, Mason told his neighbors, that lasts longer than the general good requires "may be called government, but it is in fact oppression." The best way to forestall oppression was rotation. "Whenever this is neglected or evaded . . . inevitable destruction to the state follows." Mason, however, proposed to make an exception for one man. Colonel Washington, "the gentleman who, by the unanimous vote of the company now commands it," should serve without interruption, "due to his public merit and experience." Washington's experience came from his service in the French and Indian War twenty years earlier, but his character was even more important: he merited the public's trust because he could be depended on not to betray the general good.

The next month Washington left home for Philadelphia and the Continental Congress, which voted, unanimously, to assign him a larger command than the Fairfax County militia. But the contradictory impulses expressed by Mason—suspicion of leaders versus confidence in this leader—would follow Washington in his career as commander in chief. His peers were often less eager to put limits on him than he was to limit himself. Time and again, a frantic Congress loaded him with powers, which he used sparingly, or used, then gave up. He kept the military in line, quelling mutinies when they happened, averting others before they arose, and returning his commission to Congress when peace came in 1783. In London, King George III asked Benjamin West, the American-born émigré painter, what Washington would do after the war. West said he would probably go back to his farm in Virginia. His majesty replied that if he did that, he would be the greatest man in the world. Washington went back to his farm.

In 1787 he came out of retirement to attend (and, by its unanimous vote, chair) the Constitutional Convention. George Mason was also there, as another delegate from Virginia. During a discussion of the tenure of the executive, Mason spoke in favor of rotation once more. "He held it . . . as the very palladium of civil liberty" (the Palladium was a statue of Pallas Athena that supposedly protected Troy). This time Mason proposed no exceptions, though Washington was once again in the room and would obviously be elected to fill whatever executive office the convention devised.

Troy fell, and so did Mason's Palladium, for the Constitution made the president eligible for reelection. Washington was elected and reelected, unanimously. At the end of his second term, in June 1796, Thomas Jefferson, who had once been a part of the administration but who now led the opposition to it, acknowledged Washington's hold on the American mind. He wrote James Monroe that "one man outweighs" all of Congress "in influence over the people. Republicanism must lie on its oars" and "resign the vessel to its pilot." But the pilot had once again set his course for home, for Washington had been discussing his Farewell Address with Alexander Hamilton since February. The man who was never term limited voluntarily limited his own presidency, and his example was so compelling that it lasted until 1940 when Franklin Roosevelt, mindful of the world situation (and perhaps of his own ambition), broke the two-term precedent. In 1951 the nation reset it, in constitutional stone, with the Twenty-second Amendment.

But Washington was not the only founder to set precedents for officeholding. George Clinton, son of Irish immigrants, was a lawyer and surveyor in upstate New York who became a general of the militia early in the Revolution. He surprised patrician New Yorkers when he won the first postindependence race for governor in 1777; "his family and connections do not entitle him to so distinguished a pre-eminence," one sniffed. But Clinton went on to serve six straight three-year terms. He had to sweat to win campaign number six in 1792 against John Jay; only some creative ballot counting in frontier counties reelected him. Jay actually beat him in 1795. But by 1801, Clinton was back in the governorship for his seventh term. After twenty-one years as governor, he moved up to the vice presidency in 1804, a post he looked on as a "respectable retirement." He served two presidents, Jefferson and James Madison, dying in office in the spring of 1816.

An 1814 portrait by Ezra Ames makes Clinton look big-nosed and beefy, like a Tammany Hall boss of days gone by. But he was more than a hack. He was a capable wartime leader in a state that had a rough war. He strongly opposed the Constitution when it came up for ratification in 1788, and though he lost that fight, the grudgingness of New York's approval helped convince Madison that the document needed a Bill of Rights (Clinton's allies suggested thirty-two amendments). In 1811, in the vice president's role as president of the Senate, Clinton cast the most important vote in the history of his office, breaking a tie over a bill to renew the charter of Alexander Hamilton's Bank of the United States. He voted no, following Madison's old argument that the bank was unconstitutional, although Madison himself, who was now president, had changed his mind and wanted the bank to continue. Clinton's vote was principled and disastrous, ensuring that the United States would begin the War of 1812 with empty pockets. George Clinton was a sincere patriot, as wary of oppression as George Mason. He was determined, however, to guard the general good himself, and he was so good at winning and holding office that he became known as "the Old Incumbent."

If a founder wanted to choose between George Washington and George Clinton, he had to choose between the arguments for their respective positions. Mason made the argument for rotation at the Constitutional Convention: leaders "should at fixed periods return to that mass from which they were at first taken, in order that they may feel and respect those rights and interests which are again to be personally valuable to them." This was an argument from human nature: since we are all equal, let every man remember that he is no better than his fellows. Oliver Ellsworth made the pithiest case for reelection: the executive "will be more likely to render himself worthy of it if he be rewardable with it." This was also an argument from human nature: we all have passions, including our passions for fame and power, and the state should use them as incentives to make us behave better than we otherwise might. One view admonishes human nature; the other tries to work with it. Neither is obviously wrong.

Did the Founding Fathers Cut Backroom Deals?

Sure they did; that's how we got Washington, D.C., and national prosperity.

In June 1790, Thomas Jefferson, the secretary of state, ran into Alexander Hamilton, the secretary of the treasury, outside President Washington's house on Broadway in New York City, then the capital of the United States. (The house is long gone, as is every other vestige of the early federal government. All that remains in Lower Manhattan is Fraunces Tavern, where some of the founders ate, and St. Paul's Chapel, where many of them worshiped.) "Hamilton," Jefferson recalled later, "was in despair. . . . He walked me backwards and forwards before the President's door for half an hour." One of the key planks of Hamilton's fiscal program was that the federal government should assume the debts of the states; like a TV ad with an 800 number for bankruptcy, he offered one easy monthly payment. But this plan had been voted down in the House. Some members feared that it would make the federal government too powerful, by making it the holder of too many IOUs; some wanted better terms for crediting the debts of their own states. Most of these skeptics were southerners, including Hamilton's former best friend, now all of a sudden his critic, James Madison. So Hamilton needed to talk with Madison's real best friend, Jefferson. "I told him," Jefferson went on, "that I was really a stranger to the whole subject. . . . I proposed to him, however, to dine with me the next day, and I would invite another friend or two [that is,

Madison] and I thought it impossible that reasonable men, consulting together coolly, could fail, by some mutual sacrifices of opinion, to form a compromise."

This was pure Jefferson: hospitality as statecraft. He held his dinner at his lodgings, and Madison indicated that he was prepared to give in on the assumption of state debts. "But it was observed that this pill would be peculiarly bitter to the southern states, and that some concomitant measure should be adopted, to sweeten it a little to them." That measure turned out to be moving the nation's capital from New York to Philadelphia for ten years, then to a site, as yet undeveloped, on the Potomac. "So the assumption was passed." America would become a wealthy, fiscally sound nation, with its capital in an unholy swamp.

Jefferson's little story raises some questions. It was written years after the fact; we have no memories of Hamilton's or Madison's to check it against. It is also written as self-justification. Soon after their deal Jefferson would become an inveterate enemy of Hamilton and his whole fiscal edifice, yet by his own testimony he had played a key role in setting it up. He saves himself retroactively only at the cost of making himself seem uncharacteristically stupid: how credible is it that Thomas Jefferson would be "really a stranger" to any important subject? Yet this self-portrayal makes Hamilton, by contrast, seem satanically wily. Better to play dumb if you can make your enemy out to be Dr. Evil.

Jefferson also does not mention that Hamilton gave Virginia, his and Madison's state, a better balance on its debts; that might make the Virginians seem too venal. He particularly does not discuss the main reason, besides regional patriotism and money, that Virginians would be anxious to move the capital to the Potomac. New York, though it was a slave state, already had abolitionist stirrings (the New-York Manumission Society had been founded, by Hamilton and John Jay, among others, in 1785). Pennsylvania, the other state contending for the capital, was a free state, and Philadelphia had many active Quaker abolitionists. It was irksome for southern gentlemen to bring their slaves to such environments. When George Washington served as president in Philadelphia, he found it necessary to rotate his slaves back to Mount Vernon every six months since, if they stayed any longer, they would, by Pennsylvania law, be automatically freed. (At the end of his second term, he left his last staff of slaves behind him, thus discreetly freeing them; retirement foreshadows death, and he must have been thinking of his legacy.) If the capital were in Virginia or Maryland—slave states with no abolition movements—such awkward questions would not arise.

So this deal, like all deals, had aspects that were sleazy. But it also shows one of the virtues of politics. Call it practicality, call it wisdom. No one gets everything he wants in this world; good politicians make their choices, and get what they can.

The deal was done in a dining room, if not a back room, because that's where some deals have to happen. In a short time, Jefferson, Hamilton, and Madison would be engaged in furious journalistic controversies, telling the world one another's secrets, some of them true, others made up. But when important things are on the table, sometimes the doors have to be closed.

Were the Founding Fathers Poll Driven?

No one in the founding era was interrupted at dinner by some stranger asking his opinion of current events. Yet public opinion could be gauged, by demonstrations, by memorials—letters to politicians from citizen groups—and by newspapers. (Some founders thought measuring public opinion was all a newspaper was good for: "Like a thermometer," wrote Fisher Ames, "it will show what the weather is, but will not make it better.") The founders disagreed, however, about how public opinion should be expressed, and what weight to give it.

In the summer of 1794 President Washington had a rebellion on his hands. Alexander Hamilton's whiskey tax, long unpopular on the frontier, had produced an actual uprising in western Pennsylvania. Rebels raised a flag with six stars, for the six angriest counties, burned a tax collector's house, and threatened to burn Pittsburgh. When autumn came, Washington sent thirteen thousand militia over the Alleghenies to put the rebellion down, which was done almost bloodlessly.

Washington reacted so strongly because he believed that once people started picking and choosing what laws they would obey, "anarchy and confusion" would result. He also knew whom to blame for the trouble. America had seen a proliferation of Democratic Societies—political clubs that supported the French Revolution and the Republican Party (even in the late eighteenth century, *Democratic* was not yet a universally popular totem word; by using it, the Democratic Societies were ahead of the curve). Many of the leading whiskey rebels had belonged to local Democratic Societies. When Washington reported to Congress in November on the uprising, he blasted "certain self-created societies" that had taken it upon themselves to condemn the whiskey tax.

In Washington's speech, *self-created* is a sneer adjective, like *so-called*, and it strikes us as odd. What is the matter with a "self-created" society? Isn't American public life full of them, from NARAL to NORML to the NRA? Washington saw it differently, though. In his mind the will of the people expressed itself primarily through elections, and then through the decisions of their representatives. Washington believed in political journalism—one visitor to Mount Vernon saw ten newspapers on his table—even if he didn't always like what he read. But when people formed pressure groups to lobby for or against laws, they seemed to him to be usurping a constitutional function.

James Madison, who listened to Washington's speech as a member of the House, disagreed. He was in an awkward political position. His Republican Party opposed the whiskey tax, but found the rebellion appalling and embarrassing—it was bad, and bad for the Republican Party. Madison didn't want the House, however, to join Washington in attacking self-created societies. He argued that they weren't that dangerous: "They will stand or fall by the public opinion. . . . In a republic light will prevail over darkness, truth over error—[I have] an undoubted confidence in this principle." He denied that the government had any power to criticize them: in republics, "the censorial power," or the power to criticize, belongs to "the people over the government," not to "the government over the people." If the government started criticizing, where would it stop? It might end up curtailing freedom of speech and of the press. Madison wanted to dissociate himself and his party from thoughtless, radical allies, but he was also groping toward a notion of organized public opinion. Sometimes self-created societies expressed public opinion. When they did, they would flourish. If they drifted away from it, they would fall. The House narrowly endorsed Madison's position.

Madison spoke both as a theorist of republican government and as an operative in the Republican Party. He opposed the current president, Washington, and would oppose the next one, John Adams. Meanwhile, he had to maneuver his party into a position where it might win the presidency and control of Congress. The Republicans triumphed in the election of 1800—and the shoe was then on the other foot. Madison's enemies might organize public opinion on their own to oppose him. This happened in Thomas Jefferson's second term, in December 1807, when Jefferson, and Madison, now secretary of state, proposed an embargo on foreign trade (Britain and France had been bullying American shipping, and to avoid going to war with them, we stopped trading with them). Years later, Jefferson was still talking about how New England and its merchants had reacted. "How powerfully did we feel the energy of this organization in the case of the embargo? I felt the foundations of the government shaken under my feet by the New England townships. . . . [T]he organization of this little selfish minority enabled it to overrule the Union." The rest of the country seemed powerless to make itself heard. "What would the unwieldy counties of the Middle, the South and the West do? Call a county meeting, and the drunken loungers at and about the court-houses would have collected." The embargo was repealed after little more than a year.

Sometimes public opinion is what people think; sometimes it is what they are made to think. Sometimes it's a groundswell; sometimes it's smoke, mirrors, and spin. Once you admit it into your political calculations, you accept the burden of sorting and shaping it, even as your rivals do the same.

Could the Founders Ever Have Imagined a "Permanent Campaign"?

The phrase "permanent campaign" was coined in 1980 by journalist Sidney Blumenthal to describe the life of political consultants and gurus who cycle through the careers of a shifting cast of candidates, whom they guide and outlast. But it also evokes our sense that presidential elections have become eternal. There is no gap between the World Series and spring training. The moment a president takes the oath of office, his would-be successors begin lining up speaking engagements in Iowa and New Hampshire. It is natural to assume that the founders would have seen this as madness. The first national political convention did not happen until 1831, late in the lives of the very last founders; primaries were not held for another half century.

Except that one founder had a front-row seat for a presidential campaign that lasted eight years. When James Monroe won the presidency in 1816, it looked as if Thomas Jefferson's hope that political parties might end had been fulfilled. Monroe's opponent, Rufus King, would be the last Federalist candidate to run for president. He carried only three states, and Federalism, as a national organization, finally expired. Ideology died with partisanship. Monroe, who had begun his political life as a radical Republican—he thought James Madison was too soft—had mellowed. Gouverneur Morris, a die-hard Federalist only a year earlier, expressed the general mood: "Let us forget party, and think of our country." The frantic politics of the War of 1812 seemed to have ended in peace and unity.

Yet only one man could live in the White House, and five men wanted to be that man after James Monroe stopped living there. Three of them were in Monroe's cabinet—Secretary of State John Quincy Adams, Treasury Secretary William Crawford, and Secretary of War John Calhoun. Speaker of the House Henry Clay was fourth, and General Andrew Jackson, victor of the Battle of New Orleans, made five. These were all younger men (J. Q. Adams was John Adams's son), successors to the greatest generation of the founding. But since Monroe was reelected without opposition in 1820, they had a long time to wait for their inheritance. They spent it in ceaseless scheming, which made Monroe's presidency interesting, and helped make it consequential.

The home stretch of their contest coincided with the most important act of Monroe's career, the rollout of the Monroe Doctrine. By the early 1820s, Latin America was in revolt against Spain, and in Europe, the Greeks were shaking off the Turks. In America, the permanent campaigners asked how these crises could help them. Clay, looking for opportunities to run foreign policy from the House, favored liberty everywhere, like a modern neoconservative, and urged Monroe to encourage all the world's rebels. Calhoun predicted that the reactionary powers of Europe would send troops to the Western Hemisphere to prop up Spanish rule, and advised Monroe to make an alliance with Britain to hold them off; in that event, he would control War Department patronage. Jefferson, in his Monticello skybox, agreed about Britain. "With her on our side," he wrote Monroe, "we need not fear the whole world." We might also, he added, pluck Cuba for ourselves.

The course Monroe and Secretary of State Adams picked was a mixture of firmness and restraint: Europeans should stay out of our hemisphere; we would keep them out ourselves, without Britain's help; in return, we would let Europe mind its own affairs. What Adams got out of this policy mix, besides thwarting Clay and Calhoun, was a chance to show that he was anti-British; why a son of John Adams needed to do such a thing may not be obvious, but in the regional stereotyping of the day New Englanders were always suspected of Anglophilia. What Monroe got out of it was a policy named for him.

Monroe spelled out his doctrine to Congress in December 1823.

In the wars of the European powers, in matters relating to themselves, we have never taken any part, nor does it comport with our policy to do so. It is only when our rights are invaded, or seriously menaced, that we resent injuries, or make preparation for our defence. . . . [W]e should consider any attempt [by Europeans] to extend their system to any portion of this hemisphere, as dangerous to our peace and safety.

In threading the needle of his feuding heirs, the last founder president shaped American foreign policy for decades. Only Washington's Farewell Address was equally influential.

The permanent campaign also affected Monroe personally, since it almost got him beaten up. During the last winter of his second term, Crawford came to see him at the White House. Crawford, who had led the pack for seven years, was fading; he had suffered a stroke; tension was high. He wanted Monroe to approve some picks for customs officers (Treasury's main patronage treat). Monroe objected. Crawford said something cross; Monroe told him so. At that, Crawford got up, shook his cane at the president, and called him a "damned infernal old scoundrel!" Monroe grabbed the fireplace tongs to defend himself, and threatened to have the servants throw his treasury secretary out. Crawford calmed down enough to leave under his own power, luckily for Monroe; Crawford had once killed a man in a duel.

The permanent campaign ended in 1824, when Adams beat Jackson, Crawford, and Clay (Calhoun having decided to bide his time as vice president) in a race of pure malice, without the ballast of a single idea. Monroe joined Madison, Jefferson, and John Adams where all the surviving founders (except Chief Justice John Marshall) then lived, on the Olympus of retirement.

The founders didn't have Dick Morris or Karl Rove, C-SPAN or Fox, PACs or Web sites. But they knew, from their own

experience, that politics is like water, and seeps through every
crack it finds.

Did the Founders Think That Politics Could End?

Politics is a game, which is why those who don't play it laugh at
it, but it is also a civilization, setting limits and imposing order.
As a politician, you may play hard ball, yell, lie (up to a point),
cheat (if you don't get caught), even—in the founding era—kill,
so long as it was in a duel. This is at your worst; at your best you
think, inspire, lead. But does there come a point when politics is
not enough? Politics is conflict by other milder means. Did the
founders believe it ever becomes war?

Of course they did. They were revolutionaries. Patrick Henry
laid down the marker. In 1765, England passed the Stamp Act—a
tax on American legal documents. The offense was not the fee,
though it was onerous, but who levied it—not the colonies themselves, acting in their own assemblies, but Parliament in London.
Henry, a brand-new member of the Virginia House of Burgesses,
gave a warning. "Caesar had his Brutus, Charles the First his
Cromwell, and George the Third . . ." Brutus stabbed Caesar,
Cromwell beheaded Charles. Cries of "Treason!" interrupted
Henry's sequel. "And George the Third," he swept on, "may
profit by their example. If this be treason, make the most of it!"
Was Henry so cunning that he had foreseen the outcry, and held
the retort in reserve? Or was he playing off his outraged colleagues? When you rap at that level, it is impossible to tell, and it
doesn't matter. Henry had invited his fellow lawmakers and their
sovereign to contemplate a new prospect.

When Samuel Adams was a student at Harvard, he debated

the proposition that it was "lawful to resist the supreme magistrate, if the commonwealth cannot otherwise be preserved." That was a schoolboy exercise, an academic reflection of England's Glorious Revolution of the century before. As an adult, Adams brought revolution to New England. He started small, because his resources were small and the provocation, though great in the scale of injustice, was local. During the crisis over the Stamp Act, he began to influence the neighborhood gangs of Boston, which historically had rioted against each other and safely remote hate figures like the pope. Inflamed by his rhetoric, they burned the home of Thomas Hutchinson, the colonial lieutenant governor. Adams publicly deplored the deed, sponsored a summit meeting of the gangs, and got them even more firmly under his control. In 1768 Britain sent three regiments to garrison the unruly city; two years later soldiers fired on an unruly crowd, killing five. Adams's propaganda made this famous throughout the colonies as the Boston Massacre. He then encouraged his cousin John to defend the soldiers in court, to show how moderate the colonists could be—when they chose.

Revolution came to America. The founders were traitors. The British captured three signers of the Declaration when they captured Charleston, South Carolina, in 1780 (Thomas Heyward Jr., Arthur Middleton, and Edward Rutledge), and they did not draw and quarter them, or even hang them, as traitors in other parts of the empire had been served. But on another occasion they captured Richard Stockton, a signer from New Jersey, and held him in such a vile cell that his health was broken; he died a few years later.

The war ended British rule in America, but not revolution. Massachusetts, desperately trying to liquidate its war debts, imposed a property tax so crushing that in 1786 farmers in the western half of the state broke up courts administering foreclosures. Their leader was Captain Daniel Shays, a Revolutionary War veteran. Most of the founders were appalled by Shays's actions. Henry Knox called his followers "desperate and unprincipled men." Abigail Adams called them "ignorant, wrestless desperadoes." George Washington, in retirement at Mount Vernon, called them "insurgents," and advised that "if they have *real* grievances, redress them if possible. . . . If they have not, employ the force of the government against them at once." Thomas Jefferson, following the crisis from Paris, wasn't so sure. "We have had thirteen states independent for eleven years [he wrote in 1787]. There has been one rebellion. That comes to one rebellion in a century and a half, for each state." (A part of Jefferson's mind, eager to control the world by measuring it, was always reaching for a calculator.) "What country before," he went on, "ever existed a century and a half without a rebellion? And what country can preserve its liberties, if its rulers are not warned from time to time, that this people preserve the spirit of resistance?" Then he struck off one of those images that become mythical as soon as they are written. "The tree of liberty must be refreshed from time to time, with the blood of patriots and tyrants. It is its natural manure." Six years later, Bertrand Barère, a French politician, spoke of blood-drinking trees in a speech calling for the execution of Louis XVI. "The tree of liberty . . . flourishes when it is watered with the blood of all varieties of tyrants." Perhaps the idea came to both men from ancient mystery religions, which had a vogue as a scholarly subject in Paris just then. But how a thought is phrased is as important as the thought itself. Jefferson, who returned to America in 1789, seems never to have met Barère, but they had acquaintances in common. Had Jefferson's image found its way into common talk? In 1995, when Timothy

McVeigh was arrested for the Oklahoma City bombing, he was wearing a T-shirt with the tree-of-liberty slogan on it. He got it straight from Jefferson.

In 1794 an excise tax on distilled spirits provoked a rebellion in western Pennsylvania. The first violent confrontation pitted two Revolutionary War veterans against each other—John Neville, the tax collector, and James McFarlane, commander of the local militia. Neville's house was burned down, and McFarlane was killed. This time Washington was in a position of authority, president of the United States, and he had no doubt what to do. He sent a commission to investigate (and to give any moderates a chance to cool off), then sent an army five times larger than the one he had led across the Delaware to the Battle of Trenton, over the Alleghenies. He acted from concern for republican legitimacy. Congress had passed the excise; western Pennsylvania had congressmen. They had lost the debate on the issue. Maybe they would win one day. But until then they had to obey the law.

At the end of the Adams administration, Virginia Republicans feared that the army, mobilized to repel a French invasion, might be sent against them. Why not? The federal government had taken upon itself to punish sedition. Indeed, Alexander Hamilton, second in command of the army under Washington, toyed with the idea: perhaps Virginia, he wrote Theodore Sedgwick, a senator from Massachusetts, should be put "to the test of resistance." What would Virginia Republicans have done in that case? In 1814, John Randolph, a Virginia congressman, challenged James Monroe, who had been governor of their state at the time, to say what he and other Virginia Republicans had been contemplating. "Ask him what he would have done . . . ! He *can* give the answer." Randolph later answered the question himself: "The grand armory at Richmond was built to enable the State of Virginia to resist by force the encroachments of the then administration upon her indisputable rights." An aura of craziness always glimmered around Randolph, and he was needling Monroe when he revealed what he claimed were their old plans. But it is certainly true that both Federalists and Republicans were reckless and desperate at the end of the eighteenth century, though neither the army nor the arsenal was ever used.

There is no doubt about what some Federalists planned during the Jefferson administration. Senator Timothy Pickering (a Federalist from Massachusetts) had been a colonel in the Revolution, and Washington's secretary of war and of state. (Pickering's proximity to greatness did not make him humble; he thought Washington was a dolt, and the rest of his fellow founders dolts or villains. The only one he admired was Hamilton.) Pickering and other New England Federalists so disliked life under President Jefferson that they discussed a secession of their states, and asked Jefferson's alienated vice president, Aaron Burr, if he could pull New York out of the union with them. Burr showed guarded interest. Hamilton was horrified when he learned of these discussions; the only things worse in his mind than Virginia Republicans were Burr and disunion. It was Pickering's plot that goaded him to his final quarrel with Burr. Pickering shelved his plot when his coconspirator killed his idol.

What if the government actually sent the army on an evil mission? The War of 1812, reluctantly declared by President Madison, struck New England and New York Federalists as disastrous. Gouverneur Morris wanted no part of it. "Let the present party carry on *their* war, and to that effect lay *their* taxes. Let a vain people writhe under the tyranny of *their* loving friends. Such blockheads are neither worthy of nor fit for a free government."

Like Pickering before him, Morris wanted New England and New York to secede; the man who drafted the Constitution proposed tearing it up. "It seems to me I was once a member of Congress during a revolutionary war. . . . We once had hearts—hearts that beat high with the love of liberty."

In his references to the Revolution and liberty, Morris hints at the key question for all rebels, criminals, and tough talkers, from Patrick Henry to Timothy McVeigh. What are the right grounds for revolution? Theorists had discussed the matter for centuries. The second paragraph of the Declaration of Independence offers a formula. (The words show Jefferson's gift for sweep, pith, and music, but the thought was not his alone. The Declaration was a corporate act, edited and approved by the Continental Congress. The Congress bent, folded, and spindled much of Jefferson's text, to his chagrin, but they signed off on his essay on revolution without comment, because they all accepted it.)

Governments "are instituted" to secure the safety, happiness, and inalienable rights of men. They should also take their powers "from the consent of the governed." These are the ends and means of just government. When any government "becomes destructive" of these ends, the people may "alter or . . . abolish it," so long as they intend to put a just government ("new guards for their future security") in its place. These are necessary conditions for right revolution. But there are others: the evils of the existing government must not be "light or transient"; only "a long train of abuses," aimed at "absolute despotism," will suffice. One more thing has to happen: the rebels must "declare the causes" that motivate them ("let facts be submitted to a candid world"). Revolution must be for rights, it must be against pitiless oppressors, and it must be done in public. If the rebels do all the right things, and their enemies do all the wrong things, then revolution is justified.

Note that the Constitution, written eleven years later, offers no halfway houses to revolution. It is idle for governors to stock arsenals, as Randolph accused Monroe of doing, or for states to secede, as Pickering dreamed of doing, and the Confederacy did, under the impression that they are tiptoeing within the penumbra of the law. The Constitution would be the founders' best effort—the second try, after the Articles of Confederation, modified by ten quick amendments—to secure the blessings of liberty. If the rulers it empowers become deliberately and irredeemably oppressive, then it is time to burn the house down.

CHAPTER 11

Conclusion

 $\mathcal{T}$ HIS BOOK has been asking the founders a lot of questions. Maybe the last question it should ask, by way of conclusion, is, *What would the founders think of this book?*

They might well give it, and all the other books of the founders' revival, an attentive read, for they were obsessed with posterity and fame. In 1788, George Washington was writing a letter to his dearest, and perhaps only true, friend, the Marquis de Lafayette. (It was characteristic of his lonely eminence that his friend had to be twenty-five years younger than he was, and a foreigner.) Washington strayed into what, for him, was a rare subject: epic poetry.

[The] antient bards [were] both the priests and door-keepers to the temple of fame. And these, my dear Marquis, are no vulgar functions. . . . In some instances by acting reciprocally, heroes have made poets, and poets heroes. Alexander the Great is said to have been enraptured with the poems of Homer and to have lamented that he had not a rival muse to celebrate his actions. Julius Caesar is well known to have been a man of a highly cultivated understanding and taste. Augustus was the professed and magnificent rewarder of poetical merit, nor did he lose the return of having his atcheivments immortalized in song.

On Washington marched, through the history of heroes and poets, up to the reigns of Louis XIV and Queen Anne, that is, just before he was born. Then, he broke off—"I hardly know how it is that I am drawn thus far"—and changed the subject, filling Lafayette in on the struggle to ratify the Constitution, which had reached a crucial stage: seven states had ratified, nine were needed to make it the law of the land. If the Constitution went into effect, none doubted that Washington would be the first president—republican successor of Alexander and Anne. He had not changed the subject at all.

The founders cared for the future and the opinion of the future. Yet so does every despot. My name is Ozymandias, king of kings, says Shelley's tyrant from his monument. The founders' concern was different, because their opinion of men was different. The Americans who would look back on them would, if they did their work well, be like the Americans of their own time: fellow citizens, fit to pass judgment, not just in gossip and nursery rhymes, like slaves throughout history, but in books and editorials and ballots. They submitted themselves, in death as in life, to a jury of their peers.

Yet if the Americans of the future, that is us, are the peers of the founders, that changes our relationship to them. The founders are a lively bunch, especially for men who have been dead for two centuries, well suited to intellectual give-and-take. But perhaps we should question them less. John Adams had an inkling of this. He would not like this book (though he would surely read it, and fill the margins with objections as lengthy as the text) because he saw no reason for the future to honor the founders. At least that is what he told Josiah Quincy, a young politician, when he was an old man. "I ought not to object to your reverence for your fathers, . . ." Adams wrote. "But, to tell you a very great secret, as far as I am capable of comparing the merit of different periods, I have no reason to believe we were better than you are." The critic Harold Bloom writes about the anxiety of influence in literature: the pressure poets feel from the achievements of great predecessors—Whitman, Shakespeare, the Bible—beating down on their backs. Speaking as a politician, Adams was telling the next generation to get over it. They would do their thing as well as John Adams had done his. Adams with his combination of painful self-doubt and grotesque vanity was the last man among the founders actually to be indifferent to how the future would see him. His advice is in part a defense, a way of sparing himself the anxiety of being underrated (if nobody thinks of us, nobody will think that Benjamin Franklin was better than I was). Yet he also, as he often did, had hold of a truth. The founders of a republic cannot expect that their handiwork will stand by itself. A government in which power flows from the people needs their best efforts, in every generation, to thrive.

As this book has shown, the founders shared certain big convictions, and ways to frame questions, which we can profit from. The first goal of their statecraft was liberty. Liberty drove them to independence, and to remake and amend their government after independence had been won. They knew that liberty had to be channeled in laws and institutions, and they tinkered with theirs endlessly; if they did not make every effort to secure this particular blessing, they believed they would be false to human nature. The founders believed their efforts and their country were favored by God. (Even Thomas Paine, who derided every Christian doctrine and lowercased every religious term, wrote respectfully, and with capital *A*s, about the Almighty.) They believed, with equal fervor, that the country must prescribe no particular faith.

The founders' America was not a rich country, but they sensed that it would be. Sometimes they worried that wealth would corrupt it. Yet they were reluctant to give the government too much power over economic activity in the name of virtue, or anything else, because they knew that control over money was a time-tested tool for controlling men. Only a few founders understood the new economic world that would lead from spinning jennies and banks to computers and the WTO; they were lonely in their knowledge, but since they were given responsibility for America's finances at crucial points, they guided us into our future.

The founders expected America to grow to continental size, give or take three or four million square miles (they never did get Canada). They knew this would not be an easy process. They lived among wars, local and global; they invaded other countries, and they were invaded. Their world was a violent place, and even the most pacific of them acknowledged that there would be times when they would have to be violent themselves. "Men are ambitious, vindictive and rapacious," Alexander Hamilton warned in *Federalist* no. 6. "Is it not time to awake from the deceitful dream of a golden age" and realize that we "are yet remote from the happy empire of perfect wisdom and perfect virtue?" He could have spared his warning; most of his peers were wide awake.

The founders believed passionately in educating both children and adults. Free people needed information and principles (principles suited to free government, of course: neutrals in the political wars need not apply to be professors, or journalists). They extended their concern for education, in theory and at times in practice, to women, whom they saw as mothers and first teachers of citizens, though when women on occasion participated in politics directly, they were not dismayed. Men and women who were not white drew the shortest straw when it came to education, and everything else, though this contradicted the founders' principles, and a few of them worked to correct the injustice.

They lived and died—some of them (for example, Hamilton) quite literally—by politics. Some of their own political innovations, such as partisanship, shocked them, but the game of politics always drew them in, for it was the means, dirty or inspiring, by which they secured liberty, prosperity, strength, and every other public good.

These are principles, promissory notes to principles, and civic habits that have served us well since the late eighteenth century, and will until the twenty-eighth century, if we last so long. But, as this book has also shown, the founders do not answer all, or even most, of our questions. They can't because they couldn't answer all of theirs. Or they had too many answers: they disagreed among themselves, sometimes within themselves (James Madison keeps a regiment of scholars busy trying to find the elusive point from which all his contradictory positions line up). They disagreed about taxes and spending, farming and city life, trade, immigration, and the courts. They disagreed about specific wars and peace treaties, and about which countries should be allies or enemies. Beyond the boundaries of the First Amendment, they could not agree whether to shake religion's hand or keep it at arm's length. They disagreed about democracy. "I am not among those who fear the people," Thomas Jefferson boasted when he was in his seventies. The nation's "real disease," Hamilton wrote in the last letter of his life, "is DEMOCRACY." (Not coincidentally, Jefferson's party, now called the Democrats, still exists, whereas Hamilton's party, the Federalists, barely outlived him.) They disagreed about slavery. "They are without a slave" to help them, a Hamilton family friend wrote pityingly in June 1804 as the Hamiltons prepared to throw a party at their Manhattan summer house. Jefferson died July 4, 1826, owning 130 persons who were sold off six months later, along with Monticello, to pay his debts.

They have passed these disagreements, and the disposition to disagree, on to us. Contention is as much a part of their legacy as their principles. It fills our public space, and our minds. Mere ambition generates conflict in times of peace and prosperity, and the world provides enough real problems to give us serious things to quarrel about. Slavery, for example, still exists in parts of the Muslim world, while democracy has just begun to exist there (some question whether democracy still exists here). We vehemently disagree about these matters—what we might do about them, whether we should do anything at all—just as we disagree about all the other unfinished business of the founding, and our own brand-new problems.

What we can always take from the founders, whether we are honoring the letter of their law, or improvising madly, as they sometimes did, is a style of thought, a way of working, a stance.

We can be as intelligent as they were, and as serious; as practical, and as brave. We can know as much as they did, and work as hard. We can compromise when we have to, and kill when we must. We can; as they said, all men are created equal.

Founderblogs

Welcome to *Carnival of the Founders*, a sample of some of the best blogs posted by the founding fathers. Almost all of these blogs are written under pseudonyms—some eighteenth-century habits die hard!—but Carnival has ID'd the authors for you.

Dirtyoldman (Benjamin Franklin)

Jokes, drinking songs, drinking games. Sex, some fart humor. No XXX, but pretty funny stuff. Video streams of BF singing his own songs are the best.

Keytech (Benjamin Franklin)

Innovations in science and technology. Lots of buzz on nano-technology (hat tip: Instapundit). Sidebar debunking psychics.

YouSucceed (Benjamin Franklin)

Think of a white male Oprah. Moral uplift, with an edge. Read this, and in three weeks you'll have my job!

PubliusReport (Alexander Hamilton)

The blog that left Arianna Huffington and Mickey Kaus in the dust. AH gives his opinions on politics, law, economics, foreign policy, you name it. Fastest reax in the blogosphere; either he has a twin brother (Jefferson would say an evil twin brother) or he really does know everything.

PubliusRetort (James Madison)

Everything that's wrong with *PubliusReport*. JM and AH started blogging together, but fell out (see FAQs on both sites).

FromtheMountain (Thomas Jefferson)

The simple life at Monticello. Martha Stewart for gents. Politics never crosses his keyboard. (He did advise JM to change the name of *PubliusRetort* to *FreePeople*.) The weekly wine column, Rhone Ranger, is especially popular.

TheLifeCareerOpinionsandWritingsofJohnAdamsExamined andDefendedwithCommentsonhisContemporaries (John Adams)

Long URL, even longer posts. How that man finds the time to blog it all! Eternity must agree with him. Don't miss the flame wars in the Comments; Adams frequently appears as a troll on other sites (*PubliusReport* and *AgeofReason*).

RemembertheBitches (Abigail Adams)

Same as above, more or less, but meaner. Wonkette, MoDo—forget it. This lady rocks and rules.

BeerandLiberty (Sam Adams)

Kos, Atrios, Moveon—move over. When *BeerandLiberty* blogs, people take to the streets. A little heavy on conspiracy theories (forget the Bush family and the Nazis, do you know their ties to the House of Windsor?). Hard drinking tips by Hitch and Taki.

AgeofReason (Tom Paine)

The only blog that didn't have to change its name. Paine's journo synapses still firing strong. Anti-Christian polemics; contradictions of the Bible (or, as he puts it, bible). Dr. James Dobson has called this the worst blog in America.

Toujoursfidele (Gouverneur Morris)

Midnight rambling in high society. Don't let your wife/girlfriend read it. If she's smart and you're ignoring her, she's probably in it.

Toujours-Fidele (Marquis de Lafayette)

Don't confuse with the above! All idealism, all the time. Lafayette began fighting for liberty when he was 19 years old (see About Me page), and he's still doing it 230 years later. This is the Frenchman the blogosphere loves.

Note: George Washington Sent the List Administrator the Following E-mail

While I am deeply sensible of the honor of your request that I submit a Web log (though I deny that my daily thoughts or doings would possess any interest to the generality of readers), I must regretfully decline, the pressure of business quite filling up all my intervals of leisure.

I am deeply interested in the success of your project, however, believing as I do that the discussion of ideas is an essential element in the political happiness of our country, and I look forward to reading whatever productions you are able to post online.

Your obedient, humble servant,
GWashington

Notes

The founders used footnotes sparingly—which was good for John Adams, since he might otherwise have had to acknowledge that large chunks of his theoretical writings were plagiarized. I assume every reader can find quotations from the Declaration of Independence, the Constitution of the United States of America, and the King James Bible.

Abbreviations

AH Hamilton, Alexander. *Writings.* New York: Library of America, 2001.

BF Franklin, Benjamin. *Writings.* New York: Library of America, 1987.

FC McClellan, James, and M. E. Bradford, eds. *Debates in the Federal Convention of 1787 as Reported by James Madison.* Richmond: James River Press, 1989.

FP Hamilton, Alexander, James Madison, and John Jay. *The Federalist Papers.* New York: New American Library, 1961.

JM Madison, James. *Writings.* New York: Library of America, 1999.

TJ   Koch, Adrienne, and William Peden. *The Life and Selected Writings of Thomas Jefferson.* New York: Modern Library, 1944.

W   Washington, George. *Writings.* New York: Library of America, 1997.

Chapter One: Introduction

2   "sustain his policy" Stern, 581.

3   "the architects" King, 102.

5   "will be celebrated" Butterfield, Friedlander, and Kline, 139, 142.

5   "without first asking" Shelton, 19.

5   "Had he lived" Longmore, 204.

6   "visible and palpable" Nevins, 360.

8   "middle class humbugs" Padover, 411.

9   "a medicine necessary" TJ, 413.

9   "the basis of our own" Davenport, 2:533.

10   "I have written" Ames and Allen, 1:726.

10   "will be open" FP, 36.

Chapter Two: Their World, Our World

14   "A great number" A. C. Morris, 2:244.

15   "When my Companion" Butterfield, Friedlander, and Kline, 24.

15   "[M]ankind can never" TJ, 580.

16   "black men fought" Macaulay, 3:220.

16   "a vast and bloody" H. Adams *(Jefferson)*, 1135.

17 "the enemy of" Brandt, 232.

18 "It might be" Faust and Johnson, 385.

18 "Do not lend" W. H. Adams, 9.

18 "buried alive" Bailyn, 8.

19 "At the time" BF, 1379–80.

21 "the celebrated" FC, 258.

22 "Everyone knows" TJ, 606.

25 "Curse on his virtues!" Quintana, 46.

25 "It is impossible" FP, 71.

25 "The virtues" Dryden and Clough, 1:325.

25 "In my judgment" Dryden and Clough, 1:460–61.

26 "one united people" FP, 38.

26 "Here is everything" Butterfield, Friedlander, and Kline, 79.

26 In 1785. Gaustad, 36.

27 "every accent" BF, 1409.

28 "These portions" Paine, 15.

28 "Pericles, in compliance" FP, 54–55.

28 "Those who hold" FP, 79.

28 "I was surprised" BF, 1389.

29 "ever felt the solid" TJ, 403.

Chapter Three: Liberty and Law

32 "Is it not absurd" Beccaria, 112.

32 "too many crimes" Malone, 270.

33 "exhibited as a public" TJ, 48.

33 "nothing relating" TJ, 34.

33 "the mere domestic" FP, 118.

34 thirty-nine lashes. Stahr, 277.

34 "happy . . . lenity" W, 417.

35   "Examples however severe" Bobrick, 440.
35   "barrier . . . to protect" Blackstone, 246.
36   "A well regulated Militia" Halbrook, 83.
36   "due restrictions" Blackstone, 245.
37   "A brace the more" TJ, 463.
37   "While this gives" TJ, 375.
38   anal sex. Davenport, 1:341.
39   "I wish, my dear Laurens" AH, 58.
39   "I lay most stress" AH, 60.
40   "taken familiarities" Palmer, 92.
40   "Mr. Jenifer is" Farrand, 3:93.
41   "He's pissed" BF, 267–70.
42   "But this conversion" BF, 939.
42   28 gallons of rum. Flexner, 1:211.
43   "There appears" R. B. Morris, 331.
43   "liberty of the Cudgel" BF, 1153–54.
44   "one continued tempest" McCullough *(Adams)*, 537.
45   "a few prosecutions" Brookhiser *(Hamilton)*, 202.
45   "right of freely" JM, 590.
45   "a sickly confederation" JM, 648.
45   "We have been careful" Goebel, 831.
46   "may safely be trusted" TJ, 576.
46   "brings on the sleep" TJ, 629.
47   "consult . . . dead subjects" Burrows and Wallace, 387.
48   "Good God!" AH, 6.
49   "Energy in the executive" FP, 423.
49   "take any system" R. B. Morris, 158.
50   "in the nature of a republic" Montesquieu, 124, 126.
51   "league of friendship . . . perpetual" Rossiter, 351–60.
52   George Read. FC, 206.
52   "no more subject" FP, 245.

52   "are in this country" AH, 614.

52   "Extend the sphere" FP, 83.

53   "Some such tribunal" FP, 245–46.

53   "interpose for arresting" JM, 589.

53   "interpose [their] own authority" Dwight, 361.

54   "It seems to me" A. C. Morris, 2:564.

55   "When statutes contradict" Goebel, 383.

55   "Whenever a particular" FP, 468.

56   "An act of the legislature" Marshall *(Major Opinions)*, 88.

56   "They are in the habit" TJ, 84.

Chapter Four: God and Man

59   "Whereas true religion" Brookhiser *(Washington)*, 154.

60   Benjamin Franklin. Van Doren, 550.

61   "An expression" TJ, 719.

61   "Do you not think" Bobrick, 202.

61   "that bountiful . . . my steps" Brookhiser *(Washington)*, 146.

62   "We have been assured" FC, 204.

62   "no character of enmity" H. Miller, 1082.

63   "by the indulgence" W, 767.

63   "that every person" W, 834.

64   "dispose us all" W, 526.

65   "when I expect" BF, 1179–80.

65   "Of all the dispositions" W, 971.

66   "free government" W, 971.

66   "loaded with misery" TJ, 395.

66   "I contemplate" Jefferson, 16:281–82.

67   "a happier place" W, 740.

67   "in modern day parlance" Ellis *(Sphinx)*, 259.

67   "I have performed" TJ, 632.

68   "religion in a family" Alexander, 176–77.

68   "the happy opportunity" Alexander, 176.

68   "It was asked" Wells, 158.

68   "What is it" Paine, 822, 825.

69   "sinking man" Paine, 823.

69   "a warm friend" Paine, 415.

69   "If I do not believe" Paine, 417.

71   "harmless plaything" Vaughn, 59–60.

72   "drank deeply" AH, 746.

72   "irreligion" Ames and Allen, 2:1385.

72   "an *Atheist* in religion" AH, 924.

72   "Our friend, the present President" Paine, 415.

72   "irritable tribe of priests" TJ, 558.

73   "I must explain" TJ, 697.

73   Madison expressed. FP, 77–84.

Chapter Five: Money and Business

76   "I think the Parliament" W, 155–56.

77   "the most precious" Brookhiser *(Hamilton),* 54.

77   "the national debt" AH, 535.

77   "I cannot consent" H. Adams *(Madison),* 114.

78   "If the laws" W, 874.

78   "real scarcity" FP, 223.

79   "The consumption of ardent" AH, 563.

79   "wring emotion" John C. Miller, 402.

80   "Whenever the government" AH, 915.

80   "Those who labor" TJ, 280.

81   "The life of the" JM, 511–12.

81	"Ay, but I don't" Brookhiser *(Adams)*, 34.
82	"The spirit of enterprise" AH, 664.
82	"When all the different" AH, 663.
82	"would draw forth" A. C. Morris, 2:318–19.
83	"I have not" TJ, 621.
84	"their manners and principles" TJ, 280.
84	"The tailor" Adam Smith, 424.
84	"The principles of" Ames and Allen, 1:638.
85	"a long list" Bowling and Veit, 64–65.
85	"it does not appear" JM, 818.
85	"whose right and duty" JM, 823.
86	"In every country" FC, 132–33.
86	"we have no paupers" TJ, 649.
86	"more miserable" Brookhiser *(Washington)*, 181.
87	"The earth is given" TJ, 389–90.
87	"Early to bed" BF, 1296–1302.
88	"THIS BUILDING" Weigley, 83.
88	"though the mental" Paine, 627.
89	"Is it then better" Paine, 629.
89	"His sense of honour" Paine, 622.
90	"The bowels" AH, 666.
90	"impolitic to set" Paine, 636.
91	"did not hesitate" TJ, 607.
91	"The General sent" Brookhiser *(Washington)*, 49.
92	"When I see this" A. C. Morris, 2:129.
92	"assist commerce" AH, 919.
92	"None . . . do more honor" JM, 716.
93	"Jews and Judaizing" Cappon, 134.
93	"I was derided" Cappon, 424.
93	"The necessary secrecy" AH, 598.
93	"It is a well established" AH, 577.

94 "The keen, steady" AH, 602.

94 "deadly hostil[e]" H. Adams *(Jefferson)*, 389.

94 "the hoary winter" Cappon, 599.

95 "too few to merit" TJ, 649.

95 "was the price" W, 523–24.

95 "Providence has placed" Stahr, 238.

95 "among those who will" W, 1023–24.

96 "The advantages" AH, 552–53.

97 "The proper funding" AH, 569–70.

97 "[W]hen the credit" AH, 532.

97 "If we consider" Jefferson, 17:448, 449, 456.

Chapter Six: War and Peace

102 "everything that was" W, 365.

103 "The sufferings and distress" Rhodehamel, 654.

104 "very splendid" Zachs, 29.

105 "this demonstration" JM, 710.

105 "Could it not be" Nester, 114.

106 "two blankets" Fenn, 88.

106 "I could not suppose them" Washington, 4:157.

106 "in the woods" Martin, 241.

107 "An ounce of prevention" BF, 239.

107 "I found a number" Martin, 16–17.

108 "every town to provide" Washington, 4:143.

108 "Congress ha[s] a right" H. Adams *(Madison)*, 1093.

108 "odious" Adams *(Madison)*, 1092.

109 "an important acquisition" AH, 996.

110 "set of men" FC, 351.

111 "maniac tyranny" TJ, 655.

111	"Oh, that I" Butterfield, Friedlander, and Kline, 69.
111	"You must pay" Elkins and McKitrick, 572.
111	"The finger of destiny" Brookhiser *(Adams)*, 137.
113	"peace, commerce and honest" TJ, 324.
113	"'Tis our true policy" W, 975.
113	"'Tis folly" W, 975–76.
113	"[I]nveterate antipathies" W, 973.
113	"The nation, which indulges" W, 973.
114	"I have always" AH, 523.
115	"The predominant motive" Lind, 32.
115	"Rather than it should" TJ, 522.
115	"painfully interesting" O'Brien, 253.
115	"entangling alliances" TJ, 324.
115	"we must marry ourselves" Ellis *(Sphinx)*, 206.
115	"To intermeddle" Zachs, 43.
116	"We have the greatest" Fischer, 278–79.
117	"disgraced and lost" FC, 190.
117	"We shall disappoint" FC, 228.
117	"all the advantages" Rossiter, 358.
118	"a mere matter" H. Adams *(Madison)*, 528.
118	"Prussians, Austrians or French" Bobrick, 334.
119	"disinterested attachment" TJ, 600.
119	"Here, by fighting" Szymanski, 30.
119	"offer my services" Brookhiser *(Morris)*, 65–66.
120	"support the growth" *Facts*, 26.
121	"pure democracy" FP, 81.
121	"a great beast" Knott, 73–74.
121	"our real disease" AH, 1022.
121	"Is this" FC, 134.
122	"into two parties" TJ, 715.
122	"I dread the reveries" AH, 521.

123–4   "I have never feared" TJ, 495.

123   "like a vicious" Brookhiser *(Morris)*, 320.

123   "they who are against" BF, 224.

124   "for the King's use" BF, 1415–16.

124   "I hope it will" BF, 1073.

124   "this America settles" Eastman, 986.

125   "the greatest man" TJ, 609.

125   "deluge our rising Empire" W, 500.

125   "the fate of an empire" FP, 33.

125   "we should have such" Jefferson, 12:277.

126   "We . . . have only to include" Jefferson, 12:277.

126   "neither philosophy, nor religion" Cappon, 202–3.

Chapter Seven: Education and Media

129   "reading became fashionable" BF, 1380.

130   "Fix their ambition" Cappon, 70.

130–1   "catch . . . a taste" BF, 326.

131   "the best forms" Pangle, 173.

131   "Let our countrymen" TJ, 395.

132   "form the statesmen" Kurland and Lerner, 1:689.

132   "nothing . . . can better" W, 750.

133   "Our country" W, 982–83.

133   "national feelings" JM, 717.

134   "As nothing teaches" BF, 334.

134   "chiefly performed" BF, 336.

134   "questions of right and wrong" BF, 337–38.

134   "'Tis some advantage" BF, 328.

134   "History will . . . afford" BF, 336–36.

134   "[I]n his letter" BF, 332.

135   "It is the law" Witherspoon, 78.

135   "In experience" Witherspoon, 146.

136   "makes men wiser" TJ, 433.

136   "our future connections" TJ, 430.

136   "State a moral case" TJ, 431.

136   "Fix reason firmly" TJ, 423–23.

137   "the new Prometheus" Van Doren, 171.

137   "A new appearance" BF, 795.

137   "It may be of use" BF, 897.

138   "some drug wholesome" BF, 953.

138   "The great uncertainty" BF, 1016.

138   John Adams played Cappon, 563–69.

138   "the rights of mankind" W, 517.

138   "the religion of JESUS CHRIST" Rush, 88.

139   "lordship . . . over the whole world" Locke, 180.

139   "There must be" Van Doren, 445.

140   "I hope, my Lords" Van Doren, 469.

142   "I must entreat" Brookhiser *(Washington)*, 61.

143   "Great economy might" FC, 131.

144   "[Hamilton] appoints a time" Brookhiser *(Hamilton)*, 197–98.

144   "I have sometimes" BF, 1150.

144   "How can it be believed" BF, 306.

144–5   "My arguments" FP, 36.

145   "My dear friend" A. C. Morris, 2:404.

145   "I condemn those" Hamilton, 5:124.

Chapter Eight: Men and Women

147   "There are certain" Warren, iv.

148   "Poor Gerry" Elkins and McKitrick, 556.

148   "In any other" Brookhiser *(Adams)*, 104.

149   "Then, my friend" Davenport, 1:235.

149   "anxious wishes" JM, 526.

150   "the greatest evil" AH, 752.

150   "The repose of millions" R. N. Smith, 150–51.

151   "I long to hear" Butterfield, Friedlander, and Kline, 121.

151   "We know better" Butterfield, Friedlander, and Kline, 123.

151   "If we mean" Butterfield, Friedlander, and Kline, 153.

152   "In order to spread" Wollstonecraft, 258.

152   "As I read" Lomask, 1:161.

152–3 "You reflect" Lomask, 1:196.

153   "inhabitants" McGoldrick and Crocco, 2.

155   "You should immortalize" Ellis *(Sage)*, 69.

155   "rambling . . . angry" Ellis *(Sage)*, 72.

155   "Monsieur was cordial" Brookhiser *(Morris)*, 164.

156   "Proceed, great chief" Hirschfeld, 89.

156   "I thank you" Hirschfeld, 92.

156   "The compositions published" TJ, 259.

156   "It is worthy" AH, 661–62.

157   "history, from the moment" TJ, 521.

157   "the bastard brat" Ellis *(Sage)*, 62.

158   "that hard-to-be-govern'd" BF, 1371.

158   "I was a little" Cooper, 12.

159   "Mr. Hamilton expatiated" Chernow, 227.

160   "If the world" Brookhiser *(Morris)*, 178.

160   "zones of privacy" *Congressional Quarterly's Guide*, 644.

161   "He talked of the heinousness" Boswell, 347.

161   "the liberty of the press" Goebel, 809.

161   "a master piece" Goebel, 839.

161   "uses the weapon" Goebel, 820.

Chapter Nine: Race and Identity

163   "Providence has been pleased" FP, 38.

164   "the judgment of heaven" FC, 479.

164   "I think a change" TJ, 279.

165   "Slavery in this country" Cappon, 571.

165   "Can the liberties" TJ, 278–79.

166   "shaking off a power" Locke, 444.

166   "be brought up" W, 1023.

166   "habits of idleness" Burrows and Wallace, 286.

167   "Whether this ceremony" Nevins, 2–3.

167   "Policy and economy" W, 540.

168   "The gradual extension" W, 541.

168   "never submitted themselves" TJ, 221.

168   "Our settlements will" Ellis *(Sphinx)*, 201.

169   "The British ministers" A. C. Morris, 2:568.

169   "a people once numerous" Marshall *(Constitutional)*, 2:312–13.

169   "distinct political community" Marshall *(Constitutional)*, 2:369.

170   "All men are born" Brookhiser *(Adams)*, 119.

170   "The benevolent creator" *Manumission Society Minutes,* Feb. 24, 1785.

170   "no measure" TJ, 595.

171   "We have some Negroes" McCullough *(1776)*, 36.

171   Cash Affrica. Walling *(Men)*, 20–23.

171   "Such a body" Walling ("Nimham's"), 2.

171   "their freedom" AH, 57.

172   "I frequently hear" AH, 56–57.

172   "I was outvoted" Brookhiser *(Hamilton)*, 42.

172   "The new-time people" Hirschfeld, 108.

173 "My mulatto man William" W, 1024.

173 "elegant chariot" Lomask, 1:245.

173 "real distinctions . . . fidelity" TJ, 256–61.

175 He died in 1806. Brodie, 522–25.

175–6 "I would not confine you" W, 555–56.

176 "a proof of attachment" FC, 400.

176 "boors" Van Doren, 218.

176 "bring with them" FC, 399.

176 "To be appointed" FC, 400.

176 "We should not" FC, 401.

177 "not wish to invite" Elkins and McKitrick, 694.

177 "the otters" Ames and Allen, 2:1468–69.

178 "the same language" FP, 38.

178 "scarce speak English" Stahr, 3.

179 "In the first place" BF, 689.

179 "What is it" Bobrick, 110.

179 "The summer soldier" Paine, 91.

179 "The God who gave us" TJ, 311.

Chapter Ten: Politics

182 "Dr. Franklin" Brookhiser *(Washington)*, 59.

183 "mutual forbearances" W, 817, 819.

183 "the baneful effects" W, 969–70.

183 "If I could not go" TJ, 460.

183 "quarrel with both" Brookhiser *(Adams)*, 48.

184 "we are all republicans" TJ, 322.

184 "sink federalism" Elkins and McKitrick, 754.

185 "atheist . . . fanatic" AH, 924.

185 "would not become me" Stahr, 361.

185 "mischievous . . . crafty" AH, 977–78.

186 "great ambition unchecked" AH, 980.

186 "restore to social intercourse" TJ, 322.

187 "The charge against me" AH, 888.

187 "It is well known" Gordon-Reed, 61.

188 "the serpent you cherished" Butterfield, Friedlander, and Kline, 274.

188 "That, Sir" Brookhiser *(Hamilton)*, 194.

190 "ought to be considered" A. C. Morris, 2:457.

190 "If we were truly brave" A. C. Morris, 2:458–59.

191 "Give the votes" FC, 384, 227.

192 Reptiles . . . sheep. Brookhiser *(Morris)*, 18–19.

192 "may be called government" Longmore, 155–56.

193 "He held it" FC, 353.

194 "one man outweighs" Elkins and McKitrick, 517.

194 "his family and connections" Lomask, 1:130.

194 "respectable retirement" Lomask, 1:332.

195 "should at fixed periods" FC, 353.

195 "will be more likely" FC, 341.

196 "Hamilton was in despair" TJ, 123–24.

199 "Like a thermometer" Ames and Allen, 2:1390.

199 "anarchy and confusion" W, 874.

199 "certain self-created societies" W, 888.

200 "They will stand" JM, 551–52.

201 "How powerfully did we feel" TJ, 661.

202 "Let us forget party" Brookhiser *(Morris)*, 323.

203 "With her on our side" TJ, 709.

203–4 "In the wars" Monroe, 14.

204 "damned, infernal old scoundrel!" Nevins, 354.

205 "Caesar had his Brutus" Bobrick, 73.

206 "lawful to resist" Brookhiser *(Adams)*, 41.

207 "desperate and unprincipled" Brookhiser *(Washington)*, 53.

207 "ignorant, wrestles desperadoes" Brookhiser *(Adams)*, 89.

207 "What country before" TJ, 436.

207 "The tree of liberty" O'Brien, 66.

208 "to the test" AH, 914.

208 "Ask him what" H. Adams *(Randolph)*, 34

209 "Let the present party" A. C. Morris, 2:544.

210 "It seems to me" A. C. Morris, 2:564.

Chapter Eleven: Conclusion

213–4 "antient bards" W, 681.

215 "I ought not" Ellis *(Sage)*, 99.

216 "Men are ambitious" FP, 54, 59.

218 "I am not among" TJ, 673.

218 "real disease" AH, 1022.

218 "They are without a slave" Brookhiser *(Hamilton)*, 176.

Bibliography

Adams, Henry. *History of the United States during the Administrations of James Madison.* New York: Library of America, 1986.

_____. *History of the United States during the Administrations of Thomas Jefferson.* New York: Library of America, 1986.

_____. *John Randolph.* Armonk, N.Y.: M. E. Sharpe, 1996.

Adams, William Howard. *Gouverneur Morris: An Independent Life.* New Haven: Yale University Press, 2003.

Alexander, John K. *Samuel Adams: America's Revolutionary Politician.* Lanham, Md.: Rowman and Littlefield, 2002.

Ames, Seth, and W. B. Allen, eds. *Works of Fisher Ames.* 2 vols. Indianapolis: Liberty Classics, 1983.

Bailyn, Bernard. *To Begin the World Anew.* New York: Alfred A. Knopf, 2003.

Beccaria, Cesare. *An Essay on Crimes and Punishments.* London: J. Almon, 1767.

Blackstone, Sir William. *Commentaries on the Laws of England.* Edited by William Carey Jones. San Francisco: Bancroft-Whitney, 1915.

Bobrick, Benson. *Angel in the Whirlwind.* New York: Simon and Schuster, 1997.

Boswell, James. *Boswell's Life of Johnson*. Everyman Library. New York: E. P. Dutton, 1960.

Bowling, Kenneth R., and Helen E. Veit, eds. *The Diary of William Maclay*. Baltimore: Johns Hopkins University Press, 1988.

Brandt, Clare. *The Man in the Mirror: A Life of Benedict Arnold*. New York: Random House, 1994.

Brodie, Fawn M. *Thomas Jefferson: An Intimate History*. New York: Bantam Books, 1975.

Brookhiser, Richard. *Alexander Hamilton, American*. New York: Free Press, 1999.

_____. *America's First Dynasty: The Adamses, 1735–1918*. New York: Free Press, 2002.

_____. *Founding Father: Rediscovering George Washington*. New York: Free Press, 1996.

_____. *Gentleman Revolutionary: Gouverneur Morris, the Rake Who Wrote the Constitution*. New York: Free Press, 2003.

Burrows, Edwin G., and Mike Wallace. *Gotham*. New York: Oxford University Press, 1999.

Butterfield, L. H., Marc Friedlander, and Mary-Jo Kline. *The Book of Abigail and John*. Cambridge: Harvard University Press, 1975.

Cappon, Lester J., ed. *The Adams-Jefferson Letters*. Chapel Hill: University of North Carolina Press, 1959.

Chernow, Ron. *Alexander Hamilton*. New York: Penguin Press, 2003.

Congressional Quarterly's Guide to the U.S. Supreme Court. Washington, D.C.: Congressional Quarterly, 1979.

Cooper, Helen A. *John Trumbull*. New Haven: Yale University Art Gallery, 1982.

Davenport, Beatrix Cary. *A Diary of the French Revolution by Gouverneur Morris.* 2 vols. Boston: Houghton Mifflin, 1939.

Dryden, John, trans., and A. H. Clough, ed. *Plutarch's Lives of the Noble Grecians and Romans.* 2 vols. New York: Modern Library, 1992.

Dwight, Theodore. *History of the Hartford Convention, with a Review of the Policy of the United States Government Which Led to the War of 1812.* New York: N. and J. White; Boston: Russell, Odiorne, 1833.

Eastman, Arthur M., ed. *The Norton Anthology of Poetry.* New York: W. W. Norton, 1970.

Elkins, Stanley, and Eric McKitrick. *The Age of Federalism.* New York: Oxford University Press, 1993.

Ellis, Joseph J. *American Sphinx.* New York: Alfred A. Knopf, 1997.

_____. *Passionate Sage.* New York: W. W. Norton, 1993.

Facts on File. New York: Facts on File, 2005.

Farrand, Max, ed. *Records of the Federal Convention.* 3 vols. New Haven: Yale University Press, 1966.

Faust, Clarence H., and Thomas H. Johnson, eds. *Jonathan Edwards: Representative Selections.* New York: Hill and Wang, 1962.

Fenn, Elizabeth A. *Pox Americana: The Great Smallpox Epidemic of 1775–82.* New York: Hill and Wang, 2001.

Fischer, David Hackett. *Washington's Crossing.* New York: Oxford University Press, 2004.

Flexner, James Thomas. *George Washington.* 4 vols. Boston: Little, Brown, 1965–1972.

Gaustad, Edwin Scott. *Historical Atlas of Religion in America.* New York: Harper and Row, 1962.

Goebel, Julius, Jr., ed. *The Law Practice of Alexander Hamilton.* New York: Columbia University Press, 1964.

Gordon-Reed, Annette. *Thomas Jefferson and Sally Hemings.* Charlottesville: University Press of Virginia, 1997.

Halbrook, Stephen P. *That Every Man Be Armed: The Evolution of a Constitutional Right.* 2d ed. Oakland, Calif.: Independent Institute, 1994.

Hamilton, Alexander. *The Papers of Alexander Hamilton.* Edited by Harold C. Syrett. 27 vols. New York: Columbia University Press, 1962.

Hirschfeld, Fritz. *George Washington and Slavery.* Columbia: University of Missouri Press, 1997.

Jefferson, Thomas. *The Writings of Thomas Jefferson.* Edited by Andrew A. Lipscomb and Albert Ellery Bergh. 20 vols. Washington, D.C.: Thomas Jefferson Memorial Association, 1903–1904 (known as the Memorial Edition).

King, Martin Luther, Jr. *I Have a Dream: Writings and Speeches That Changed the World.* Edited by James Melvin Washington. San Francisco: HarperSanFrancisco, 1992.

Knott, Stephen F. *Alexander Hamilton and the Persistence of Myth.* Lawrence: University Press of Kansas, 2002.

Kurland, Philip B., and Ralph Lerner, eds. *The Founders' Constitution.* 5 vols. Chicago: University of Chicago Press, 1987.

Lind, Michael, ed. *Hamilton's Republic.* New York: Free Press, 1997.

Locke, John. *Two Treatises of Government.* New York: New American Library, 1965.

Lomask, Milton. *Aaron Burr.* 2 vols. New York: Farrar Straus Giroux, 1979.

Longmore, Paul K. *The Invention of George Washington.* Berkeley and Los Angeles: University of California Press, 1988.

Macaulay, Thomas Babington. *Critical and Historical Essays Contributed to the Edinburgh Review.* 3 vols. London: Longman, Brown, Green, and Longmans, 1854.

Malone, Dumas. *Jefferson the Virginian.* Boston: Little, Brown, 1948.

Manumission Society Minutes. From the Collection of the New-York Historical Society.

Marshall, John. *The Constitutional Decisions of John Marshall.* Edited by Joseph P. Cotton Jr. 2 vols. New York: G. P. Putnam's Sons, 1905.

———. *Major Opinions and Other Writings.* Edited by John P. Roche. Indianapolis: Bobbs-Merrill, 1967.

Martin, Joseph Plumb. *Private Yankee Doodle.* Eastern Acorn Press, 1991.

McCullough, David. *John Adams.* New York: Simon and Schuster, 2001.

———. *1776.* New York: Simon and Schuster, 2005.

McGoldrick, Neale, and Margaret Crocco. *Reclaiming Lost Ground: The Struggle for Woman Suffrage in New Jersey.* New Jersey Historical Commission, 1994.

Miller, Hunter, ed. *Treaties and Conventions Concluded between the United States of America and Other Powers since July 4, 1776.* Washington, D.C.: Government Printing Office, 1889.

Miller, John C. *Alexander Hamilton: Portrait in Paradox.* New York: Harper and Brothers, 1959.

Monroe, James. *The Monroe Doctrine.* Boston: Old South Leaflets, 1823.

Montesquieu. *The Spirit of the Laws.* Translated and edited by

Anne M. Cohler, Basia Carolyn Miller, and Harold Samuel
Stone. Cambridge: Cambridge University Press, 1989.

Morris, Anne Cary. *The Diary and Letters of Gouverneur Morris.*
2 vols. New York: Da Capo Press, 1970.

Morris, Richard B. *Alexander Hamilton and the Founding of the
Nation.* New York: Dial Press, 1957.

Nester, William R. *"Haughty Conquerors": Amherst and the Great
Indian Uprising of 1763.* Westport, Conn.: Praeger, 2000.

Nevins, Allan. *The Diary of John Quincy Adams.* New York:
Longmans, Green, 1928.

O'Brien, Conor Cruise. *The Long Affair.* Chicago: University of
Chicago Press, 1996.

Padover, Saul K. *Karl Marx: An Intimate Biography.* New York:
McGraw-Hill, 1978.

Paine, Thomas. *Collected Writings.* New York: Library of
America, 1995.

Palmer, John McAuley. *General Von Steuben.* Port Washington,
N.Y.: Kennikat Press, 1966.

Pangle, Thomas L. *The Ennobling of Democracy.* Baltimore: Johns
Hopkins University Press, 1992.

Quintana, Ricardo. *Eighteenth Century Plays.* New York: Modern
Library, 1952.

Rhodehamel, John, ed. *The American Revolution.* New York:
Library of America, 2001.

Rossiter, Clinton. *1787: The Grand Convention.* New York:
Macmillan, 1966.

Rush, Benjamin. *The Selected Writings of Benjamin Rush.* Edited
by Dagobert Runes. New York: Philosophical Library, 1947.

Shelton, Charles M. *In His Steps.* Springdale, Pa.: Whitaker
House, 1979.

Smith, Adam. *The Wealth of Nations*. New York: Modern
    Library, 1937.
Smith, Richard Norton. *Patriarch*. Boston: Houghton Mifflin,
    1993.
Stahr, Walter. *John Jay: Founding Father*. New York: Hambledon
    and London, 2005.
Stern, Philip Van Doren, ed. *The Life and Writings of Abraham
    Lincoln*. New York: Modern Library, 2000.
Szymanski, Leszek. *Casimir Pulaski, a Hero of the American
    Revolution*. New York: Hippocrene Books, 1994.
Van Doren, Carl. *Benjamin Franklin*. New York: Viking Press,
    1938.
Vaughn, William Preston. *The Antimasonic Party*. Lexington:
    University Press of Kentucky, 1983.
Walling, Richard S. *Men of Color at the Battle of Montmouth*.
    Highstown, N.J.: Longstreet House, 1994.
_____. "Nimham's Indian Company of 1778." East Brunswick,
    N.J.: [n.p.], 1999.
Warren, Mercy Otis. *History of the Rise, Progress, and
    Termination of the American Revolution, Interspersed with
    Biographical, Political, and Moral Observations*. Boston:
    Manning and Loring, 1805.
Washington, George. *The Writings of George Washington from the
    Original Manuscript Sources, 1745–1799*. Edited by John
    Clement Fitzpatrick. 39 vols. Washington, D.C.:
    Government Printing Office, 1931–1944.
Weigley, Russell F., ed. *Philadelphia: A 300-Year History*.
    New York: W. W. Norton, 1982.
Wells, William Vincent, ed. *The Life and Public Services of
    Samuel Adams Being a Narrative of his Acts and Opinions, and*

of his Agency in Producing and Forwarding the American Revolution. Boston: Little, Brown, 1865.

Witherspoon, John. *An Annotated Edition of Lectures on Moral Philosophy*. Edited by Jack Scott. London and Toronto: University of Delaware Press, 1982.

Wollstonecraft, Mary. *A Vindication of the Rights of Woman, with Strictures on Political and Moral Subjects*. New York: Scribner and Welford, 1890.

Zachs, Peter. *The Pirate Coast*. New York: Hyperion, 2005.

Acknowledgments

Alexander Hamilton was walking down Broadway one day with his wife when they passed a vet who was hawking copies of George Washington's Farewell Address. Hamilton told her that the man wanted him to pay for his own words, since he had ghosted the address—a fact that did not become public until long after Hamilton died.

The founders were thrifty with acknowledgments, but I am pleased to thank Richard Snow and Linda Bridges for their thoughts and help, and especially my wife, Jeanne Safer, who gave me the idea for this book and its title.

I would also like to thank my editor, Elizabeth Maguire, and my agent, Michael Carlisle.

Index